CHANGE

How Understanding Personal Origins Can Help Leaders Navigate Change

Dr. Jessica Spallino

Copyright © 2020 Jessica Spallino

All rights reserved.

No part of this book may be used or reproduced in any manner or format without written permission of the author, except in the case of brief excerpts for review.

The information provided within this book is for general informational and educational purposes only. The author makes no representations or warranties, express or implied, about the completeness, accuracy, reliability, suitability or availability with respect to the information, products, services, or related graphics contained in this book for any purpose. Any use of this information is at your own risk.

info@jessicaspallino.com

First Edition

ISBN: 979-8556948822

I dedicate this book and the enlightening personal work it represents to those that have taught me the most about myself and my deepest purpose: Mom, Dad, Joe, Julie, Jim, Jon, Isabella, Ashlyn, Josh and Mark.

Acknowledgements

It has been a long journey getting to this point in my life to share a compilation of personal experiences, painful and joyous, along with a developed viewpoint on a topic I find both personally fulfilling, and which has the capacity to make a significant difference in our lives and the world around us. My deepest origins lie with my family: my mom and dad, who did the best they knew how to do, along with my courageous and infinitely thoughtful siblings. Though we don't choose our origins, and many create struggle throughout our lives, they have helped me become aware, strong, compassionate, and in a position to share my story and perspective. For those we do choose, I thank my beautiful and extraordinarily kind and caring daughter for all she continues to teach me, and my patient husband, who leads me to the light each and every day. Those that have acted as mentors throughout my life are the teachers I desperately needed. They've each guided me during critical times throughout my life and have taught me how to care for myself and others. And to those that brought this topic to light in my life, mired in their origins, I thank you. Without key experiences with change resistance, I wouldn't have committed to looking deeper and working to unravel the complexity of our origins and how they can keep us from finding peace and contributing to change in our lives and the world around us.

Contents

Introduction 1

Chapter 1: Personal Origins and Change 5

Chapter 2: Leading Through Change: TRACK and into SHIFT 13

Chapter 3: Phase 1: Destructing the Old Norm 31
    Stage 1: Turmoil 31
    Stage 2: Regret 45

Chapter 4: Phase 2: Constructing the Norm 61
    Stage 3: Adjustment 61
    Stage 4: Commitment 75
    Stage 5: Keep 89

Chapter 5: Origin Stories 101

Chapter 6: SHIFT: Leader in Action 121

Chapter 7: Planning for Change 153

Epilogue 161

List of Tables 165

References 167

Recommendations for Additional Reading 171

Index 173

Introduction

"The nation will find it very hard to look up to the leaders who are keeping their ears to the ground."
—**Winston Churchill**

I often marvel at how I developed a passion for a topic as prevalent as change. For most of us, change is simply a part of everyday life. Whether voluntary or involuntary, things change; we grieve, adapt, and move on. A friend, relative, or spouse dies, we lose a close friendship that we valued, a disruptive change occurs at work, or our organization reorganizes. Really, what more is there to go on about? My roots in a tumultuous upbringing and as a renegade in one of my previous organizations have created a lifetime of challenges in maneuvering change gracefully and effectively. Additionally, my innate compulsion to develop an understanding of why things occur and the need for resolve has generated a path to deeper insight on how to enact change effectively. The combined characteristics derived from both my nature and nurtured experiences have drawn me to the topic of change not only to solve my problems and desire to know more about change, but to extend the insight I've gained through my own experiences to others in the hope of helping guide them through change within themselves, their communities, organizations, and the world around them.

Throughout the many years I have spent in counseling and healing, I have grown accustomed to searching for the root cause of responses in their various forms throughout my life in order to ensure the destructive ones are dealt with at their core. Often, if I'm not successful in finding the root cause, then the adverse reaction will continue to emerge until it is dealt with directly. Throughout my life, I have found that these roots, or origins, are established within every one of us, and they drive our behavior and response to change. I propose that we cannot address change within ourselves, in others, within communities or institutions, without becoming aware of and addressing these origins. Complaining about a new boss is one thing, but the ability to look deeper at why there may be resistance to the new boss and understanding how to address it allows us to set the stage for authentic change to take place in all areas of our lives and our world. When we discover the key to unlocking the barriers to change, life begins to have a much deeper meaning and purpose.

Looking deeper for origins at play during change is an investment well worth the time and effort for the change to be successful. Observing and responding to how these origins in ourselves and others impact change efforts and inform how we behave is essential during any change. Dismissing this valuable process can impede needed and meaningful change and alter natural and necessary changes in our lives. Whether voluntary or involuntary, the stages of change I've developed and appropriately named as acronyms, TRACK and SHIFT, are outlined in this book to help navigate the change process and keep sharp awareness of the ways in which origins interact with the change. If the change is voluntary and set to move forward, it can be futile without a plan in place. Many voluntary change efforts are defeated by resistant origins that weigh down the entire process and destroy any chance for the change to be possible. Preparedness for the variance of origins throughout each stage of the change can help participants and leaders dissolve undesirable origins that are often persistent for lifetimes and create barriers to change.

This book has served as a profound psychological exploration of change in my life and how it can apply to change in others' lives. Combined with research and practical experience, my goal is to not only come to terms with many of my own origins and the obstacles they create during change, but to help others going through the same process. My hope is that this book makes the process of change not only less tumultuous, but personally enlightening. I share deeply personal stories of change throughout my life to provide concrete examples of where our origins "originate" and how they inform our reactions throughout our lives.

The format of this book may require somewhat of an adventurous temperament, as it navigates through personal and practical narratives. As you read through the chapters, you will advance through transitions from personal stories I share from my childhood and beyond to assist in demonstrating the construction of an origin and how it encapsulates a specific feeling or stage that is identified as part of the TRACK common stages of change. Each stage of change proposed throughout this book is at first exemplified through a personal story and then translated into the specific TRACK stages of change from the change participant's perspective.

From there, I share the key finding of leadership as the primary determinant of successful change based on my research on human response to change and apply those findings to describing stages of change from the leader's perspective. Numerous examples of leaders within a variety of fields are shared with a direct focus on the origins they each bring to change they have accomplished. An approach to planning for change is designed and discussed to inform any leader or participant navigating or pursuing change. The following chapters demonstrate a deep and comprehensive look at change, how our origins impact change efforts and how to navigate it conscientiously and effectively.

Chapter 1: Personal Origins and Change

Many of my childhood memories with my family are at the horse races. My dad was a compulsive gambler and would often insist our family of seven join him during his visits to the track. Though it often invited spirited criticism, I always chose the horse with the prettiest and boldest-colored uniform to win. I especially liked the way the bright contrasting colors of the horse blinders and saddle pad cloths coordinated with the jockey's uniform. Occasionally, my dad would allow me to place a $2.00 bet, which would always be on the horse whose colors stood out the most, though my strategy was rarely successful. My dad, however, won often. Throughout his fifty years of gambling on horses, he always won big or lost big. I have endless memories of touring the Southern California racetracks with my family. Each track had its entertaining features to keep all five of us kids happy while my mom and dad spent their day betting on horses.

At home, I was sometimes given the job of walking down to the liquor store to buy the racing form, which my dad would diligently study in preparation for our day at the track. Sometimes we didn't mind being forced to go, as racing day usually meant the day started out with my dad in a pretty good mood, tolerant, and kind of fun to be around. He always made sure we had money for food and depending on the location of the track, we'd be let loose for the day to entertain ourselves. This meant spending the day in the nearby mall, playing at the beach, or keeping ourselves busy in the infield.

A long day at the track could also get boring, and out of fatigue we'd often end up in the stands, which was usually around the time of the last race. It was exciting when my dad took me with him to bet on the last race and he would let me hold the tickets. If it was a bad day, we all knew it the moment we arrived. It was as if the tension and darkness had a seat of its own among us. My dad would barely say a word, as he seemed hypnotized while chewing on the corner of the race program.

We all knew to sit down and be as inconspicuous as possible. If I hadn't been able to help place the bet, I would peer over his shoulder to catch a glimpse of his tickets, so I knew who I'd be praying for to win. Once the race began, the tension would sink to the pit of my stomach, and I'd find myself firmly repeating the horse's number under my breath. I'd watch my dad for cues on whether it looked like his horse had a chance to win. Toward the end of the race, I'd jump to my feet and join the others in the stands, screaming hysterically for his number to win. Once the horses passed the finished line, we all knew the drill.

Despite the outcome, our family's race to the car began as the last horse crossed the finish line. If my dad had a win, the race to the car was a bit delayed from cashing in the winning ticket, followed by a slightly more jovial sprint. If he had a loss, the race to the car was survival of the fittest. If you were injured or slow, you could very likely be left behind to fend for yourself. My dad always led the race; he walked so quickly he was essentially running. The race to the car was the only time my mother ever ran, and she would struggle to keep up with him, followed by us five kids frantically trailing behind. My mom would periodically turn and firmly shout to us to keep up in a tone completely contrary to her usual demeanor. She sounded like a wild mother antelope bleating to her babies as they fled an advancing predator. She ran, grabbing my youngest brother's hand, who was unaware of the intense race underway.

Once we made it to the car, the relief from having secured a ride home was short-lived. We immediately began preparing for the ride home, the tenor of which always corresponded with my dad's luck that day. If the last race furnished a win, then the drive home would often lead to a stop at the local Kmart, where we'd each be allowed to pick out any sort of treat we wanted — within reason, of course. I always opted for the standard pick: a new coloring book with crayons and a candy bar. If the last race did not furnish a win, or if the day was an overall loss, then the drive home took on quite a different mood. The atmosphere in the car was either suffocated with a strained silence or a piercing barrage of expletives, often targeted at one of the innocent passengers trapped in the vehicle for some sort of violation, such as walking through an oil puddle before getting into the car. These tirades often led to further aggression once we arrived home, and sometimes they resulted in a physical altercation, where he might aggressively handle or hit one of my brothers or even my mom. If this took place, he would often lock himself in his room for days, sometimes even weeks. Unfortunately, the mother antelope tried to watch out for us, but she couldn't always protect her young from such attacks. This type of day set the stage for the cycle of addiction throughout my childhood.

My dad was a central character and dominant influence throughout my childhood and an ubiquitous presence in my adult life. His black lunch pail with the large sticker slapped across the front ordering "Live Better, Work Union" securely attached to the back of his ten-speed bike with a weathered bungee cord will always exemplify my dad. During his 27 years of working at Southern California Edison as a lineman and union steward, he rarely missed a day (quite possibly only a couple in his career). His work ethic was as reliable as his gambling addiction.

Though never officially diagnosed with a mental illness or disorder, my dad exhibited characteristics of bipolar, depression, and anxiety. Mental illness, including schizophrenia, has maintained its presence in my family, and it has been a central aspect of our lives. My dad's dominant demeanor dictated the mood of our home. It was either deliriously fun and lighthearted or maniacally dark and abusive. These moods were accompanied by the corresponding treatment that was sometimes pleasant, and, other times, terrifying. Ultimately, my father's moods created an unstable and unsafe environment.

Growing up in this environment during my formative years, I learned to cope by developing the habit of continuously scanning my surroundings for clues in other people's behavior. If I anticipated what might come next, I could ensure I was adequately guarded. As a result of adopting this coping mechanism, over the years, I have often misinterpreted other people's actions and assumed the worst in a desperate attempt to save myself from getting hurt. My attempts to guard myself from change are a direct result of my origins. As a young child I was terrified of change, and as I got older I saw everything through the lens of my six-year-old-self. I used to find myself studying others during very harmless scenarios, just like I did with my dad during the last horse race of the day. I searched for any clue to know how fast I had to run back to the car to be sure I got a ride home, or I would flee to disappear and avoid it altogether, which has been my usual go-to.

The unpredictable atmosphere and precarious level of safety I experienced as a child in our home provided me a strained relationship with change that I still grapple with in many ways today as an adult. My dad had some great qualities as well, and I hold my warm memories of him very close to my heart. He instilled the value of hard work, along with prideful integrity in every one of us, and he was a true champion for the underdog. However, his passion for representing those underserved could, at times, reach the point of becoming toxic and destructive. Though his intentions were sincere, I believe it was the righteous fight that mostly drove him, and I have found that the same fighting spirit also drives me at times. I, too, have developed a passion for challenging traditional systems and striving for change. I aim to create fairness and balance with a constructive and measured approach to matters of injustice, inequality, or efforts toward change. The powerful influence my dad had on my life has played a large part in my compulsion to study how people respond to change.

This focus has led me on a path to learn more about change dynamics, and to discover why and how dealing with change can be such a deeply personal experience. We all live in a changing environment, and there is no way to avoid change in all aspects of our lives. Whether it is involuntary change, such as a shift in our work industry, living through a pandemic, losing a loved one, or a voluntary change such as changing a job, developing a healthy lifestyle, or cultivating a new relationship, we approach change in individual ways based on our personal experiences or origins. Some of us may embrace change more easily than others and some may even go as far as to seek change. Either way, we each bring a comfort level with change based on our established relationship with change, and this is the area of reflection and study that my work attempts to discover.

My lived experience and my studies in educational leadership and curriculum and instruction have led me to explore the response to change in both myself and others, and to try to understand how people can confront change more reflectively and constructively. I believe my upbringing has helped place me on an unconventional path in a variety of ways. Although I was trained as an educator, I have never worked in a traditional school environment. I have always been attracted to the more personalized and less standardized work model that fosters deep creativity and unique ways of meeting objectives that challenge the established system. Personally, my path has been far from typical. While my conditioned response to volatility has created instability in my life at times, it has also brought about many opportunities for meaningful transformation.

My continued fascination with change dynamics and the impact it has had on my life led me to pursue it as the subject of my doctoral research, and subsequently, to write this book, which has been one the most therapeutic endeavors of my life. My personal stories shared throughout this book — mired in mental illness, emotional abuse, and overall volatility — hold deep significance and influence on my journey through change. However, this book is far more than a personal indulgence. I introduce an approach to change that is holistic and personally transformational. To that end, I share my memories and stories to illustrate how our past experiences often fuel our continued reactions to change and offer a guide to approaching change with curiosity and optimism, rather than turmoil and resistance.

I hope my intimate stories will help explain my positionality to the topic of change, as well as illustrate the often-compelling human response to it. I believe our personal stories provide profound and psychological examples of the foundation that can be laid in a person's response to future situations. These situations that may "feel" similar and can cause a cascade of reactions that derail the trajectory of change in our lives. Though I am not a licensed psychologist, I aim to make the connection between these formative experiences — or as I like to call them, origins — and how they play out later in our lives as an Origin Response (OR) during dynamic change experiences.

Through my research and experience in personal and professional settings, I have observed that a person's response to change often manifests in a variety of stages. Having spent so much of my childhood in tense and potentially harmful situations, such as those at the racetrack — specifically during the last race — I have developed a sharp ability to watch for a shift or change in the environment, mood, or dispositions of others to ensure my safety. This guarded behavior has played out in my life as an adult in ways that keep me cautious during times of change or shifts in my environment, and as I've maintained an intrigue in the connection between my origins and my adult behavior during change, I've become deeply curious about origins others must be bringing to change scenarios as well.

Each stage can provoke a distinct and deep-rooted emotion, some of which is evoked by the immediate context and surroundings. In contrast, others emerge from deeply ingrained responses that were generated during formative experiences from our past.

I have categorized the change process into five stages that are common among many people, for which I use the acronym TRACK. I include personal stories that depict key emotions that often take place within each stage. TRACK provides a framework that helps us follow the stages through the change process in order to better support those navigating through it. This tracking system helps make some of the unpredictable emotions that are generated in ourselves and others during the change process become more predictable. This framework can also ultimately equip us with the awareness to prepare and support others through the sometimes-difficult stages of change. The five stages and the feelings they bring about in us are:

1. **Turmoil**: apprehension, fear of the unknown and loss of control

2. **Regret**: grief, disorientation, and confusion

3. **Adjustment**: developing a vision, communication, and tenacity

4. **Commitment**: empowerment, individualization, and creativity

5. **Keep**: revolutionize and evolution

The first two stages, Turmoil and Regret, represent the process of deconstructing the norm before the change, and the last three stages,

Adjustment, Commitment, and Keep, demonstrate the construction of the new standard per the change. Deconstructing the norm involves the sometimes-arduous process of breaking down and releasing the old way of doing things. The process of dismantling an old norm, which includes evaluating the emotions related to turmoil and regret, is not easy. Think of something as common as moving from one home to a new one and remember how you had to think at first about taking a new route from your home to and from work. Many of the first times you do it, you might drive more cautiously because you don't know the conditions of the roads as well, or you may even miss the old route because you liked to stop at the convenience store on your way. You may feel disoriented or even confused at times. All of these emotions may come up, and how you handle them may be reliant on any origins you may bring with you. You may insist on taking the old way home to your new home, even if it's not the fastest route, so that you can still take certain roads you're used to. Until you've grown accustomed to the new route and have developed a new norm, maybe even found a new stop to pick up a snack on the new route, you are still deconstructing the old norm and this takes time.

Each phase is equally critical for the change process to effectively take place. Ample time and support are needed during the change process to deconstruct what was once familiar. Often, not enough time is spent during the deconstruction phase, and this can impede change efforts. Because the deconstruction phase can be so uncomfortable and tumultuous based on origins of resistance, the stages throughout this phase can often be overlooked or not tolerated. This can cause the change process to halt during the deconstructing phase and never even make it to the constructing phase. Equally, constructing new patterns that are viable and germane are critical in ensuring the change is relevant and sustainable. The stages within this phase can also be dismissed based on a lack of awareness or patience and can deter any attempted change to successfully take. Neglect of either phase can deter any successful change, and disregard for any of the phases or stages within them would be similar to painting a dark wall white with a single coat. The color underneath would seep through and absorb the new color without several coats to ensure the new color emerges and prevails.

As I explore each stage of the change process, I share stories that illustrate a powerful emotion that has lingered with me throughout my life, which are triggered during situations that elicit that same emotion and analogous reactions during change. I believe the connections I have discovered between these ingrained emotions and how I react to the stages of the change process provide valuable information. I can more clearly understand why I respond the way I do, and I may ultimately uncover solutions to challenging responses that act as barriers to effective change in all aspects of my life.

This analytical process can be applied to anyone navigating the change process and guide deep exploration into their own origins and how they play out throughout these stages. Allowing time and attention during these stages will enable any change participant to identify and adjust the origins of resistance throughout the change process, along with maximizing their innate strengths. Informing the change process with this cognizant approach can lead to change that is not only effective and sustainable, but cultivates personal transformation that can impact overall peace and valuable experience with successful change. Once the five stages of the TRACK process are fully explored and developed, we will transform each stage into a critical step in planning for change from the perspective of a leader. This tool aims to support any individual or organization in planning for change, accounting for influential origins present throughout the process.

Chapter 2: Leading Through Change: TRACK and into SHIFT

My interest and fascination with change response led me to making it the focus of my research for my doctoral dissertation. The overall findings of the study I conducted closely align and contribute to the stages of change outlined in this book. Based on my research in an academic setting, I found that there are several aspects of change that are applicable to every person, regardless of their setting or circumstances. My research question was, how do K-12 public school educators respond to curricular change? My dissertation explored factors that contributed to successful change and to change failure. The purpose of my study was to better understand educators' experience with change during a transition in the curriculum in a variety of school settings.

For over three months I researched and observed three different K-12 educational programs. I used open-ended online surveys and conducted focus groups as data-gathering events. I worked with four participants who experienced change within their organizations and who helped oversee and contribute to a transition from a traditional textbook-based curriculum to a completely online curriculum. What follows is a summary of my research and as well as my findings.

The Significance of the Study

Change can be hard in any industry, but it can be especially challenging within the field of education. Reform in education has taken on many different forms throughout the years, from No Child Left Behind to today's Common Core Standards. However, many of these initiatives don't last, and the opportunity for real reform is lost. Some of my research reveals a cyclical pattern in reform movements. They emerge every decade or so, and then things return to the status quo, leaving the educational organizations who attempted the reform only slightly modified, and generating minimal change in overall practices and outcomes. I believe the main reason for such failed attempts at actual change and reform is that the phenomenology of change is often neglected. Failure to understand, plan for, and accommodate how educators experience change and what the change was intended to do provides insight into the failure of reform attempts.

School Programs Observed and the Research Approach

I researched a variety of school programs to demonstrate the impact change can have on different educational models. The three models researched were:

1. A standard unified school district in a high school setting, serving students in mainstream and credit recovery classrooms, along with an independent study program.

2. An independent study program operating under a school district, serving students in kindergarten through 8th grade.

3. An independent charter school serving high school students in a blended program (partial onsite and online work).

The programs I chose for my research represent alternative educational models, primarily because of their level of experimentation in curriculum formats used for students with needs of different modalities. Credit recovery, independent study, and homeschool programs tend to attract students that either need or are looking for a non-traditional approach to teaching and learning. These programs are then charged with the task of developing new ways for learners to engage in different types of learning modalities that accommodate flexible pacing and independent work. I used qualitative research in my study because it can provide an interpretive, naturalistic approach to the world, and it studies things in their natural settings, attempting to make sense of, or interpret, phenomena in terms of the meanings people bring to them.

In an attempt to better understand these participating educators' responses to the phenomenon of change, I designed a qualitative paradigm approach to examine their response to change at their organizations. The research question was not aimed at the curriculum materials, but rather the human response to the change. I believe this was most effectively acquired through a qualitative paradigm and a phenomenological approach.

Themes

Central Themes and Statements Regarding Educator's Response to Change	
Theme	Statements
Fear	Neutral: "Am I going to be successful at this?"
	Negative: "It's about the people the change is going to impact and the fear of the unknown"
Micromanagement	Positive: "No micromanagement at all, a very high level of encouragement, lots of really good suggestions"
	Negative: "I often felt like my boss monitored everything I did because he thought I wouldn't do it right"
Follow through	Positive: "It's very important that the leader isn't always solving the problems and the staff is seeing things through with their own skills"
	Negative: "Throughout the change I found myself constantly waiting to hear from leadership about this, this and this"
Change Agent	Positive: "I've been given the space to be a change agent"
	Negative: "So, the decisions were being made by everyone above with the idea that I would be the one to run it and implement it and all of that, and then nothing was really happening with it, until then it was all dumped on me"
Buy in	Positive: "Getting their feedback (teachers) for buy-in is very important"
	Negative: "Change doesn't come from the ones who just want to ease through their day and know exactly what is expected from them and don't want to do anything more and just the ones that are just comfortable"
Communication	Positive: "When the change is communicated to staff and they are included in the process of planning the change they have a vested interest"
	Negative: "I'm updating them, he's telling the superintendent, they'll update the board, so there's a lot of room for interpretation error and that's been kind of what the challenge is"
Freedom	Positive: "The change was really good and it gave the teachers a lot of freedom, and they took that freedom and ran with it"
	Negative: "as far as how often we were receiving direction – it was not very - it was just "how's the online program going?""
Trust	Positive: "There is a high level of trust that I know what I'm doing"
	Negative: "The change process has just been getting people on board and seeing the need for the change and embracing it and that's been my job"
Collaboration	Positive: "It's not a one-person show or a one-department show – it's very much collaborative and supportive of us"
	Negative: "At first it was a one-man show and I was doing everything, but realized I couldn't do everything alone"
Vision	Positive: "The vision has come from the fact they want us to give them the vision"
	Negative: "And there was never a clear direction, and one of the big things I never got was the vision."

Table 1.1 Central Themes and Statements Regarding Educator's Response to Change

To understand participants' perspectives and beliefs, I analyzed their stories through their writings and discussions. From those, I identified ten themes from open-ended survey question and focus group question responses.

Many similar responses were expressed from two participants who tended to have a more positive response to the curriculum change. In contrast, similar responses were expressed from the other two, who appeared to have a more negative response to the curriculum change. Both positive and negative statements from the participants are included to demonstrate their experience with the given theme.

The table outlines the central themes identified along with key statements gathered from the participants that signify that identified theme. It is interesting to note here that though the themes were identified based on responses from all four participants, the two that had a positive and supportive experience with leadership expressed those themes with positive statements, whereas the two participants that didn't have a positive experience expressed those themes with negative responses.

For example, Freedom is a theme that emerged based on responses from all of the participants. Those that received a high level of support from leadership stated that in regard to Freedom during change, "The change was really good and it gave the teachers a lot of freedom, and they took that freedom and ran with it." In this scenario, the leadership was able to support and empower those involved in the change and they were able to implement it with a positive outlook. In contrast, the participants that did not have a great experience with leadership during their change stated that, "As far as how often we were receiving direction — it was not very — it was just 'how's the online program going?'" Clearly, for this participant leadership did not provide enough guidance or the support to empower her with the freedom to help facilitate the change and feel positive about it. These opposing views within the same themes demonstrate just how critical effective leadership is ensure successful change.

These clusters exhibit central factors that contributed to the participants' change experience that either represented a positive or negative response. Each of these factors can fit within the TRACK stages of change and assist in identifying where an overall deficiency or breakdown takes place in the change process.

As outlined below, I then grouped the themes into clusters based on similarities and consistencies.

Clusters & Themes regarding Educator's Response to Change	
Cluster	Themes
Resistance	Fear
	Micromanagement
Empowerment	Change Agent
	Freedom
Relationship	Trust
	Communication
Standards	Buy-in
	Vision
Guidance	Follow through
	Collaboration

Table 1.2 Clusters and Themes Regarding Educator's Response to Change

Overall, ten themes emerged, many of which were expressed by more than one participant. For example, the themes encouragement, freedom, change agent, hands-off, flexibility, and vision emerged for both Participant 1 and Participant 2, as there were many similarities in their experience and response to curriculum change. Additionally, the themes fear, interference, follow-through, communication, and vision emerged for both Participant 3 and Participant 4, as their experiences were similar and more from a negative perspective.

Through the analysis of each participant's response to and perspective on change, I assigned prevailing themes and clusters to each participant, along with an identifier. As part of the Interpretive Phenomenological Process (IPA), an identifier was highlighted from the focus group transcripts that captured instances of each theme. Keywords from the transcript were extracted to exemplify each participant's overall experience with change and noted as an identifier in the table below, along with the prevailing themes and clusters per participant. Assigning each participant a cluster that best represents their overall experience with change at their organizations, along with a supporting identifier from the transcripts, helps to create a persona of sorts for four of the clusters. This ultimately helps to personalize the cluster and better understand the human response that aligns with it.

Clusters, Themes, and Identifiers regarding Educator's Response to Change			
Participant	Cluster	Themes	Identifier
Mike	Empowerment	Change Agent Freedom	"Felt supported and effective"
Leona	Relationship	Trust Communication	"Space to see change through"
Keara	Guidance	Follow-through Collaboration	"Felt alone and unsupported"
Sally	Standards/Beliefs	Buy-in Vision	"No one knew what was going on"

Table 1.3 Clusters, Themes, and Identifiers Regarding Educator's Response to Change

Finally, I identified the two key findings of Culture and Leadership through the reduction process and have outlined them in the table below, along with their corresponding clusters and themes.

Key Findings based on Clusters, Themes. Identifiers regarding Educator's Response to Change			
Key Finding	Cluster	Themes	Identifier
Leadership	Relationship Guidance	Trust Communication Follow through Collaboration	"Felt Supported and Effective" "Felt alone and unsupported"
Culture	Resistance Empowerment Standards/ Beliefs	Fear Micromanagement Change Agent Freedom Buy-in Vision	" Space to see change through" "No one knew what was going on"

Table 1.4 Key Findings based on Clusters, Themes, and Identifiers Regarding Educator's Response to Change

Key Findings

The following sections on leadership and culture describe the main factors associated with effective change that I identified in my research on change within educational organizations. Each will be examined and later applied to other change scenarios throughout this book.

Leadership

Based on all the participant's responses, leadership emerged as the most influential factor of successful change. Nearly every response provided by the participants on their experience with change could be linked to effective leadership. Many of the responses reflected a positive experience with leadership, and others expressed frustration with leadership or perceived the lack of leadership. Among all of the responses, leadership was referred to in nearly every response. The key finding of leadership is comprised of the clusters of relationships and guidance. The cluster of relationships is made up of trust, collaboration, and communication, and the cluster of guidance includes the themes of hands-off, follow-through, and flexibility.

Within any organization, everything is impacted by its leadership. Though there may be individuals or even teams that can operate effectively without strong leadership, no organization can collectively navigate through change effectively without capable leadership. Though this is not a groundbreaking finding, it reinforces and amplifies the critical need for effective leadership for any change to be successful. Authentic leadership inspires trust and confidence, and a good leader is someone worth following during the uncertainties of change.

The participants expressed similar, and at the same time very different, experiences with leadership during change at their organizations. Participants 1 and 2 both shared positive reactions to the change within their organizations and described the leadership as supportive, empowering, highly communicative, and flexible. They also expressed that the leadership was transparent about wanting to implement change, included them in the process, and encouraged them all to try new ways of doing things within the change with a genuine tolerance of failure. If the new way didn't work at first, they were empowered to keep trying. There was an overwhelming emphasis on the safety both Participants 1 and 2 felt during the change to make mistakes. They each felt that the leadership provided support within the unknown outcomes of the change and took ample responsibility for the success or failure of it and continued to empower them all to keep trying if at first they weren't successful.

Participants 3 and 4, on the other hand, did not have positive experiences, and expressed breakdowns in the support they received from leadership during change within their organization. They expressed that they felt supported at times, but the vision, guidance, and consistency often weren't present, and it left them feeling misdirected and often lost during the change. Due to a lack of overall vision and implementation follow-through, not a single step in the process was successful, and the continued misguided failed efforts began to pile up and sabotage the entire change. The teachers who were expected to implement the new program became disgruntled, support staff was frustrated, and students and their parents began to lose faith in the overall program. Before they could even begin the initial implementation phases, it was beginning to fail. Participants 3 and 4 were beginning to resent the leadership that was supposed to be supporting and empowering them. During their participation in this case study, they were still working to find ways to develop effective relationships with leadership during their change implementation.

Leadership emerged as one of the key findings that demonstrated the most critical implications discovered within the study of educators' responses to curriculum change within educational organizations. Based on the participant responses, all of the identified themes can be negatively or positively attributed to leadership. Leadership has a direct influence on all of the experiences shared by the participants.

Culture

As part of the findings of this study, acceptance or resistance to change emerged as a primary force within the cultures of the organizations, and each organization's culture exhibited traits that helped define their propensity for the proposed change. The culture of an organization encompasses the collective behavior and norms, along with the attitudes, beliefs, habits, and capabilities of its members. Though leadership is ultimately responsible for establishing and maintaining the culture within an organization, it can be influenced by individuals and groups within the organization, and of leadership doesn't make it a visible priority, it can significantly impact change efforts within an organization.

Participants 1 and 2 expressed an overall healthy attitude toward the change and a culture that supported and encouraged it. On the other hand, participants 3 and 4 expressed that they experienced an overall neglect to support others through the change and no commitment to seeing it through effectively. The key finding of culture is comprised of the clusters of resistance, empowerment, and standards, and beliefs. The cluster of resistance is made up of the themes of fear and micromanagement, the cluster of empowerment includes the themes of change agent, and freedom and the cluster of standards and beliefs are made up of buy-in and vision.

In regard to schools, daily, monthly and annual routines provide basic security and comfort with knowing what to expect. Implementing successful change can be difficult when the culture is not well developed with open communication and high expectations. All four participants shared that there were fear and trepidation within their organizations in response to the change. Many were fearful that they wouldn't be successful with the new change or wondered how it would impact their job, and others felt a lack of investment in the change, as they didn't feel a part of the change process in any way.

Participants 1 and 2 worked in an environment that was open and supportive of change. The change was actively pursued, and when it was implemented with follow-through from leadership and their respective change agents, buy-in was common among all of the staff. They also shared that not only was the vision for the change defined and communicated, but others were greatly encouraged to seek change that helped strengthen their overall program. Conversely, Participants 3 and 4 expressed the lack of communicated vision throughout the change implementation within their organizations. They approached leadership on several occasions for guidance on the vision of the change, but it was never fully developed or communicated.

Primarily, leadership is the most influential determinant of successful change based on this qualitative study. The culture of the organization and its capacity for change is often a result of the leadership in place. However, it can develop tendencies of its own based on individuals and teams within the organization. There can even be an established culture within a school or district, with opposing views from a teachers union, and balancing the two is an ongoing and, at times, arduous task for even the most experienced leaders. This study ultimately shows that leadership helps establish and build culture, and both are critical for successful change within an organization.

Leading Through Change

Collective research along with experiences I've had with change, both personally and professionally, have informed the conclusion I make that the capacity for successful change is largely reliant on the efficacy of leading through the TRACK stages of change. The ways in which our origins interact with the emotional stages of change requires aware and capable leadership. Informed with TRACK, leaders can ensure that every stage is not only considered but accommodated with strategies for support, resolution, and the ongoing cultivation of the path for the next stage. This can include individual or collective change, whether it is personal or professional. Utilizing TRACK empowers the leader in each of us to effectively navigate imminent change throughout our lives as well as leading others through a change process.

I have observed responses to change so consumed by deep rooted origins, that they destroy people's ability to be constructive and create an exorbitant amount of pain and suffering that far outweigh any discomfort the actual change may have generated. I grew up in an environment pervaded with unpredictable volatility, where there was no care for individual or collective responses, which created an overall climate of trepidation. I have also been a part of organizational change in my professional life that became so corrupted by destructive origin-driven responses to change that individuals left their jobs because the stress level was so high that they became physically ill and needed treatment.

I imagine many of us have witnessed or have been a part of tumultuous change in life or in work, and maybe it was disconcerting or we figured it was merely a part of life. Clearly, change is a part of life. From moderate to extreme change, we are responding to shifts in our lives each and every day. What is consistently lacking during either ineffective or especially arduous change is the awareness and commitment of the process through change and empowered leadership to navigate it. In the case of the educators I studied in my research on the response to curriculum change within educational institutions, it is possible to determine in which stage or stages of the TRACK change process leadership either thrived or failed to succeed during the change process.

The two participants who experienced fulfillment and success during the change implementations expressed that leadership developed a supportive relationship, which most critically takes place during Turmoil and Regret, the first two stages of TRACK. They also equally expressed the presence and feeling of empowerment, which materializes during Adjustment, Commitment, and Keep, the last three stages of TRACK, when those involved in the change are provided the tools with which to contribute to the success of the change.

However, the two participants who shared an experience weighed down with disappointment and frustration shared that the attempted change implementation lacked the development and communication of a vision for the change, which is part of the Adjustment stage of TRACK, where leaders work to develop a vision for the change, and communicate and enforce it with tenacity. In addition, they expressed the lack of buy-in, which is developed through the commitment of leadership during the last three stages of TRACK — Adjustment, Commitment, and Keep — where they generate investment in change participants through creative and individualized strategies.

While the inventory of the change participants didn't include any focus on their origins and how they may have been a part of their responses to change, it is noteworthy that the two participants who experienced success in the change they went through each seemed to possess an OR to change that welcomed change and felt comfortable in a change environment. Unsurprisingly, the two that did not experience change success appeared to have skeptical ORs to change. Whether or not the lack of leadership guidance had an influence over the perceived ORs of the participants would need to be further explored in follow up research.

Further research on the origins of the leaders and their institutions would be extremely informative on why the navigation through the change wasn't effective. Are there resistant origins within the school district itself? Do the leaders have personally held origins that prevent them from visualizing the change or supporting others through it? Responses to these questions would provide an even deeper understanding of where the breakdowns were in leading through change.

Change Adopter Categories

As a result of our personal origins, we each have certain tendencies that may reflect on our relationship with change and how we respond to it. Consider a sudden change to the flight plan of an airplane mid-flight, and how effective it is in demonstrating how people respond to change. This example not only helps to expose general categories of change adopter categories, it can assist leaders in preparing for the different level of change adopters during critical change. Imagine the ecosystem of a routine airline flight that encounters a change in the conditions as described below:

- Pilot (Leader): The pilots are leaders of the plane that deliver change initiatives along with vision and directives. They navigate extreme turbulence and make modifications to standard practices. Pilots must often adjust their settings, flight plans, and overall vision, and communicate that to their crew.

- Crew (Change Implementers): The next level of leadership on the plane is the crew, who administer directives and oversee implementations. This team provides direction and guidance to each other and to all passengers to ensure alignment with the revised practices and overall flight plan. Ideally, all are invested in the revised initiatives and vision.

- Obedient Passengers (Change Supporters): These are compliant passengers who exhibit buy-in to the change initiatives and overall vision. They are your standard passengers on the plane. They remain in their seats, keep their seat belts fastened, and comply with ongoing directives. They may even go so far as to help the crew with implementing the changes by supporting other passengers on the plane.

- Disgruntled Passengers (Change Resistors): They are resistant to the change initiatives, and express frustration through a variety of measures, all destructive to the change and overall culture. These passengers disrupt progress toward the revised flight plan by hovering by the bathrooms when directed to stay seated, requesting additional accommodations, and complaining about any inconveniences. These passengers delay order and alignment to the practices necessary to achieve the overall vision of a revised, safe flight plan.

- Those detained and arrested upon landing (Change Defiants): These passengers flat out lose all sense of reasonableness and sometimes express violent opposition to the new directives, and the crew and obedient passengers are likely required to detain them. They may even be sedated and, upon landing, be arrested and banned from the particular airline altogether.

As a leader during change, experiencing a breakdown within any category of change adopters can disrupt a change effort within any ecosystem. As a leader navigating change, relying on ongoing analysis of those being led can help identify the range of change capacity in individuals who can be called upon to help support and even lead the change efforts to those needing additional counsel. Combining the consideration of these categories of change adopters, along with supporting the variety of individualized ORs to change efforts, can help to inform preparation for navigating through the TRACK stages of change.

To summarize, change participants can be categorized as follows:

Role	Response
Leader	Lead the change
Implementors	Administer directives and oversee change
Supporters	Compliant and buy-in to the change
Resistors	Resistant to the change
Defiants	Oppose the change

Table 2.1 Change Adopter Categories

Leading Through TRACK and Then SHIFT

The TRACK stages of change are designed to inform, prepare, and empower change participants during any type of change. The SHIFT stages of change (**S**upport, **H**elp, **I**mitate, **F**ortify, and **T**ransition) aim to provide leaders with appropriate and effective steps to take to facilitate change by addressing each of the stages of TRACK. Both TRACK and SHIFT provide a framework from which to work through change for both the participant and leader. TRACK provides the stages of change commonly experienced by change participants and acts as a framework for which to better understand the emotions and themes of each stage. SHIFT focuses on the actions a leader can take in order to support change participants who are going through the TRACK stages of change. For every stage of TRACK that a participant experiences, there is an action identified in SHIFT intended to support the participant with that stage.

TRACK

TRACK Stages

	Stage	Participant	
Deconstruct the Old Norm	1	Turmoil	Apprehension
			Fear of the Unknown
			Loss of Control
	2	Regret	Grief
			Disorientation
			Confusion
Construct the New Norm	3	Adjustment	Vision
			Communication
			Tenacity
	4	Commitment	Empowerment
			Individualization
			Creativity
	5	Keep	Revolutionize
			Evolve

Table 2.2 TRACK Stages

TRACK is developed with the change participant's perspective in mind. The first phase of TRACK consists of the deconstruction process of the old norm, which is dominated by turmoil and regret and includes feelings of apprehension, fear of the unknown, loss of control, grief, disorientation, and confusion.

From the position of the participant, it is imperative to allow for the progression through these stages with tolerance and care in order to properly address and potentially resolve deeply held origins with the ranging emotions during these stages. Some ORs may be more powerful or resistant than others and may require additional attention.

To demonstrate, the table outlines the emotions commonly experienced by the participant throughout the change stages:

Throughout this book, I share personal stories that reflect my own origins and the responses they create during each stage of change. I examine the power of these origins and their impact on responses throughout my life as examples of how we can all try to make sense of ORs to potentially resolve those that create difficulty in our lives during change.

SHIFT

	Stage	TRACK: Participant		SHIFT: Leader	
Deconstruct the Old Norm	1	Turmoil	Apprehension	Support	Prepare
			Fear of the Unknown		Inform
			Loss of Control		Appoint
	2	Regret	Grief	Help	Counsel
			Disorientation		Organize
			Confusion		Confirm
Construct the New Norm	3	Adjustment	Vision	Imitate	Guide
			Communication		Connect
			Tenacity		Persist
	4	Commitment	Empowerment	Fortify	Invest
			Individualization		Listen
			Creativity		Diversify
	5	Keep	Revolutionize	Transition	Challenge
			Evolve		Transcend

JessicaSpallino

Table 2.3 TRACK/SHIFT Matrix

SHIFT appeals to a leader's perspective during change. The support a leader provides during this phase of change that encompasses emotional responses such as apprehension, grief, and disorientation is critical in order to transition to the second phase of constructing the new norm. If leadership doesn't provide adequate patience and sensitivity for a wide range of responses during the first phase, making it to the second phase becomes impossible.

SHIFT aims to provide leaders with an action-oriented response to each stage of TRACK in order to build a plan to guide others through change. The action steps of SHIFT treat the emotions and systems of TRACK in order to nurture the change and its participants as shown in Table 2.3.

After exploring the impact of ORs and how they may appear throughout change, I will transition to observing various examples of change leaders and how their origins affected their efforts and contributions towards change. From there, we will further examine the stages of SHIFT and how it can help leaders in planning or responding to any type of change among the varying change adopters.

Leadership and Change

There are a myriad of examples provided in this book to call upon while examining leadership during change efforts. Leaders willing to investigate resistance and charge forward during key transformative situations provide powerful examples as to how to deal with not only origins in others, but also navigating their own throughout the TRACK stages of change. Reflecting on myself as a leader and as a person who has experienced volatile change throughout my personal and professional life, there are many instances when my leadership abilities have been deficient and underdeveloped. As I revisit experiences where major tensions arose between myself, as the primary change agent, and those with acute origins of resistance to change, I realize there were many ways I could have done things differently and far more effectively as a leader. I could have taken the time and care to recruit interest and buy-in for the many initiatives I was pushing to change.

As I've explored and researched leadership in times of change, I have often wondered what change would have looked like within many of the critical change experiences throughout my life had I employed more developed leadership skills. I've wondered how many of the personal stories I share throughout this book may have been less damaging had the leadership in each scenario been more developed — myself included.

How might the change that I prompted in the organization in which I worked if the leadership practiced conflict resolution strategies and found ways to bring teams together toward the same vision and outcomes? How much less pain could I and my loved ones experienced had I utilized better communication and deeper awareness of leading those who needed me most? I've also wondered how different my tendencies and ORs would be today if my upbringing was equipped with family leaders better equipped to nurture through the perils of mental illness and change that occurred throughout my formative years.

Though pervaded with some remorse, this reflection ignites complete hope and inspiration in me to further develop awareness and practice toward the infinite changes ahead in my life. It also places me in a position to share what I have learned with others in hopes to help anyone looking for guidance and solutions during change resistance. I look forward to sharing my personal struggles, triumphs, epiphanies, and potential solutions in the upcoming chapters on the complex dynamics of change, starting with the first stage of TRACK.

Chapter 3: Phase 1: Destructing the Old Norm

The first two stages of change: Turmoil and Regret, represent the process of deconstructing the norm before the change is fully actualized. Counsel and support are critical during this phase to ease the emotions that arise while releasing old standards. Time and care are essential during the change process to deconstruct patterns and to support the origins of those that struggle during this phase and to successfully transition to the second phase of constructing the new norm.

Stage 1: Turmoil

Whether voluntary or involuntary, a person's initial response to change is often impaired by stress and unrest. Due to factors such as apprehension, fear of the unknown, and the feeling of losing control, this stage can transform even minor obstacles into significant barriers that make the change arduous, if not entirely impossible.

This stage can potentially generate the most anxiety of all the stages, as the unknown and losing control can cause high levels of distress and worry. Worrying interferes with any natural process in our lives and can be destructive. It not only affects our performance, but can impact our health and overall well-being. When worrying becomes chronic, it can contribute to a variety of health conditions such as elevated blood pressure, increased risk of cardiovascular disease, depressed immune system, ulcers and other digestive disorders, and changes to blood chemistry. If it is persistent, it can raise the risk of diabetes and lead to clinical depression, or reduce the ability to form lucid new memories and recall others, and even dull the sharpness of the mind. Worrying and stressing over things to come is a typical response, but it doesn't serve anyone or any effort well. Worrying about possible change can ensure its failure, which can create even more worry and stress. The combination of extreme stress and newfound change can leave one worse off than before the attempted change.

	Stage	TRACK: Participant	
Deconstruct the Old Norm	1	Turmoil	Apprehension
			Fear of the Unknown
			Loss of Control
	2	Regret	Grief
			Disorientation
			Confusion
Construct the New Norm	3	Adjustment	Vision
			Communication
			Tenacity
	4	Commitment	Empowerment
			Individualization
			Creativity
	5	Keep	Revolutionize
			Evolve

TRACK/SHIFT Matrix

JessicaSpallino

Table 3.1 Stage 1: Turmoil

Apprehension

It was a school day, and like most days, I went to my best friend's house down the street after school. I decided to go home a little early on this particular day, as I was hungrier than usual for dinner. I ran down the street and through the iron gate to our front porch only to stop suddenly upon my arrival. My mom was sitting on the front porch; she had her head down and appeared to be crying.

As a ten-year-old, I had no idea what to think other than something terrible had happened to her, and I needed to help her in any way I could. I asked her why she was sitting on the front porch crying, but she didn't reply and seemed to try and hide it all from me by deepening her cowered posture and hiding her face. Her frailty prompted a fight response in me, and though afraid, I went to the front door to go in and face what had hurt her, knowing deep down it was my dad. I tried to go in, but the front door was locked. I tried the inside door in the garage, but it was locked as well. I returned to the porch and sat with my mom until she was finally able to look up at me and talk. She still wouldn't say much, and as we sat there, we heard the lock on the front door release. Though hesitant, I went in to investigate. The Christmas tree in the family room was the first thing I saw; it was lying on the floor, and the ornaments were strewn all over the place. The dish rack on the kitchen counter was on the floor with dishes broken everywhere, and the barstools were knocked over and lying on their sides. I looked down the hallway for my father, but he had already quarantined himself in my parents' bedroom.

My mom eventually came in, and my brothers and sisters had come home as well. We worked together to clean up and restore the Christmas tree to its rightful position. I still don't know what caused the eruption, but that night as we ate bean and cheese burritos at the kitchen bar, my mom made her way down the row of us devouring our dinner, hugging each of us. She told us that night that we would be going away to live with my grandparents in Oregon. I couldn't imagine moving to Oregon or how living with my grandparents would work, but I knew whatever was going on at home felt very uncertain and scary.

My dad isolated himself in his room for over a week after the eruption. We had become used to his disappearance after a flare-up, but this was longer than usual. He would slip out the back door to come and go to work and ventured to the kitchen while we were sleeping.

I waited for further announcements on when we may be leaving, but they never came. Instead, one day I came home after being at my friend's house, and my mom and dad were peacefully watching TV in their usual spots on the couch as if nothing had happened.

Though the experience felt traumatic at the time, it was customary for us to simply move on from incidents like this as if nothing had happened until the next explosion. As I got older and became more confident, defiant, and self-assured, the outbursts became too difficult for me to sit back, be quiet, and just watch. When I was a little older, and able to drive, I once came home on a rainy afternoon to find my younger brother, who had recently been diagnosed with schizophrenia, beaten by my dad for letting the dog in from the rain. I loaded my brother into the car and drove to pick my mom up from the bus stop, where she was let off every day from work. I screamed and cried, pleading to her to do something to avoid anything like this from happening again. We drove to my paternal grandmother's house, where my mom called to arrange yet another potential move for us to my grandmother's house in Oregon.

At this point I was 17, and I had little capacity to cope with such pain and anxiety. I dropped my mom and brother off at the house and left for several days to stay with a friend and numb the pain. When I eventually returned one evening, I walked into the house to see my mom, dad, and brother seated in the living room watching TV after having dinner as if nothing had ever happened.

These recurring episodes were tumultuous and created a level of fear and uncertainty that collided with my ability to live a fully present life. The contrast of this dark version of my father with the other, more gregarious dad who took us all to the beach or on a family trip to Disneyland, created confusion and apprehension in me. As a result, my family lived in a state of wariness. In a variety of ways, my siblings and I continue to live with some form dysfunction today due to the bipolar lifestyle growing up and the feeling of apprehension to which we became accustomed. I also developed a feeling of hopelessness, as it became apparent that no change would ever take place to address the violent outbursts, and that we'd always revert back to the volatile lifestyle. I have found that the chronic anxiety I have developed sometime conflicts with living a life supportive of change.

For many of us, apprehension is a response deeply ingrained from past experiences during formative years, and that is something to consider when interacting with others during a proposed change. Even now, as an adult, certain scenarios will create that same feeling of apprehension I felt at the end of every racetrack day, and at times I default to that described feeling of dread that leads to worry and then to complete over-analysis. The over-analysis seems to be an adaptation I've developed in an attempt to desperately protect myself from a disastrous result, like my dad flying off the handle and hurting someone if his horse lost a race.

This process plays out in key relationships in my life, both personally and professionally, and requires continuous adaptation. For example, my husband and I love the outdoors, and we often enjoy mountain biking, hiking, or even just exploring. While we were dating, we'd try to get out as often as we could. My husband is an advanced mountain biker, and I was more used to hiking, so when we opted for a mountain biking afternoon, we'd usually need to select trails that could accommodate my beginner skills. One particular day, he suggested a mountain bike ride, and I amply prepared for it. Just before meeting to go on the trip, he switched it up (an everyday occurrence for him now that I know him well) and suggested a hike instead. Rather than adjusting to the simple change and putting on some hiking shoes, it somehow triggered apprehension and worry in me, and I began to overanalyze the situation. My mind raced with questions such as, "Why did he change the plans suddenly?" "Is it because he knows I'm horrible at mountain bike riding?" "Is it because he doesn't have enough time for a bike ride and wants to shorten it to a hike so he can get to whatever else he needs or wants to do?" and then "If that is the case, why wouldn't he just tell me?" and finally, rock bottom "Does this mean I can't trust him?"

Yes, a sudden change in plans with somebody I care about and want to trust could trigger a response that neurotic, and sadly, this can still occur on occasion. I believe this reaction is directly related to those racetrack experiences and the feelings they generated. This cycle of apprehension can lead to dysfunction in our lives that ultimately impedes the natural flow of change and prevent intentional change efforts. My husband and I have worked together to develop our communication so we can address this ingrained dynamic. Although I have evolved tremendously, the racetrack episode will, at times, randomly insert itself in the most trivial scenarios and adjustments need to be made.

The process of change can be so tumultuous at times that it can directly impact the potential for success in our personal and professional lives. Dismantling our automatic responses and assumptions can be an essential step to approaching change in a healthier way and increasing the odds that the attempted change will be successful. Creating time for a pause to identify whether a response is exaggerated due to our past experiences or if the reaction is just one to wrestle with until a constructive position is acquired can be useful in creating a clear path for change. I will explore this further in the Chapter 4.

Fear of the Unknown

I started kindergarten when I was four years old. Back in the early '70s there was much less worry about developmental readiness and much more concern with getting yet another child out of the house five days a week. I was the fourth out of five kids growing up in a lower- to middle-class home that was somewhat strained by mental illness and dysfunction, so it was hardly a judgment call. The decision to send me to school at the age of four was made purely from a need for survival.

On my first day of kindergarten, I sported my matching blue floral polyester top and skirt that my grandmother made. Still at home with one last pre-kindergarten child, my mom sent me off with my sister to walk to school for the first time. My older sister, a veteran of the journey, moved briskly as I trailed behind reluctantly. Once we arrived at the school, I was dropped off at what would be my new home five days a week.

I was feeling anxious and overwhelmed with fear, and I was not at all pleased with or equipped for the new location and community that had been thrust upon me. Rather than complying with the directions to move to the rug and play with the designated "wait while all the others arrive" toys, I stood at the front door of the classroom, eliciting blood-curdling screams and cries of anxiety. I lamented my homesickness for all the newcomers to enjoy.

My distressed outburst at kindergarten drop off time became a daily routine. My anxiety and fear of the new environment overwhelmed me, and I was struggling to cope effectively. I would sometimes get over the crying spell at drop off, but only to return to it upon nap time. I did not attempt to connect with others. I was miserable, and I was making others miserable as well.

Although my poor sister was consistently burdened with the responsibility of walking me to school and dropping me off each morning, my teacher finally reached out to my mom to express her concern that I wasn't developmentally ready for kindergarten. When my mom later retold this portion of the story, she said upon discussing my case with my teacher, I "miraculously" recovered and never cried again. Maybe out of necessity I finally gathered the coping skills needed to handle the anxiety and stress of the unknown.

Now, I know with certainty that I was not the only child who started kindergarten at four years old, and many children struggle with the transition to school. However, I believe the struggle many children have in this scenario is fueled by a fear of the unknown. It is an emotion many people commonly experience throughout their lives, which makes it an even more compelling emotion to explore as a response to experiencing a change in our lives.

Indeed, fear of the unknown may be the most common reaction humans have to change. Logically, when a person does not know what is coming or what the impact will be, they feel fearful, and fear can lead us to unusual, and at times, destructive behavior.

The framework called the SCARF model, developed by neuroscientist David Rock, highlights the five goals that are inherently important to the brain (aside from staying alive):

- Status: Importance relative to others

- Certainty: Ability to predict the future

- **A**utonomy: Exerting control over events
- **R**elatedness: Sense of connection with others
- **F**airness: Fair exchanges between people

According to this model, our brain prefers to be in control, and the desire for certainty is one of its top priorities. Uncertainty generates a vivid response in our limbic system and leads us to feel fear and anxiety. Uncertainty can cause us to speculate and even create a fictional story with a horrible outcome, just to feel as though we know what will happen. Additionally, by fabricating a negative result, we save ourselves the heartbreak and disappointment of suffering the worst-case scenario. Thereby, we avoid the disappointing situation we've falsely created and halt change. This cycle likely plays out throughout all of our lives in many different forms.

Like most moms who find a flexible work setup while their kids are young, when my daughter was a little one, I found a great position managing curriculum and new programs at a small charter school. My boss was supportive and allowed me to work from home in order to balance parenthood and work. I enjoyed my job and felt very fortunate to be given such accommodations, and I made sure I earned the privilege. Once my daughter was in middle school, her needs continued to change, and I was able to devote more time to work. I completed a master's degree and became a more visible and active leader at the charter school.

I worked tirelessly there to implement new programs, including a new online curriculum for students in all grades. I developed significant skills in implementing online programs, and I also gained experience fighting fierce resistance to change. Many people who held to a more traditional approach within the organization were not at all ready for some of the changes I was leading. I will describe some of these experiences further in Chapter 7.

During my time at the small independent study charter school, I quickly became the change agent, looking to improve the program we offered to students with a diverse set of backgrounds. The changes

I brought became highly controversial, based on what I perceived as resistant origins of those impacted by the change. Although the organization survived the destruction caused by acute resistance to change, critical areas of the culture were damaged, and a great deal of momentum was needed to begin rehabilitation. Struggling with the opposition took a significant toll on me, and at that time I didn't have the energy or inspiration required to rebuild it. Throughout those years, I developed professional relationships within the online curriculum companies that worked with the school, and eventually, one of them offered me a position selling their curriculum.

This point in my career, my position at the small charter school was my only professional experience outside of bartending for several years while I put myself through college. The thought of working for an international curriculum company was not only exciting, but was also a crucial step forward in my professional development.

The days following the job offer were anything but steady. Just like that four-year-old crying at the entrance of my kindergarten classroom, I felt terrified of the uncertainty that lied ahead. I spiraled into a frenzy as I considered whether to take the job. I was mired in generating potential scenarios, each new one worse than the last. I was sure I would never meet my quota because no one would ever want to purchase curriculum from someone as inexperienced as myself. I might lose the job and ultimately become unemployed, all while my husband was unemployed himself at the time. As I grappled with these fears, I began to lean toward staying at the school, rather than taking the position.

Eventually, the company issued a deadline on the proposed offer, so I had to quiet my mind and dig deep to make a bold decision. Finally, I decided to leave the school and embark on one of the most valuable professional experiences of my life. If I had continued fearing the unknown, allowing anxiety to flood my mind, and imagining the worst-case scenarios, I would have never gained the valuable experience that contributed significantly to my professional capacity and trajectory.

Loss of Control

The sound of her heartbeat kept replaying in my mind. I was in utter disbelief. Driving home from the doctor's office, I became nearly hysterical and had to pull over to the side of the road. I had been suffering from nausea during a volunteer trip to a youth camp in the mountains, but the thought of pregnancy never occurred to me. I described my illness during a brief call to my mom, and she simply stated, "You're pregnant," as if she was revealing something as matter of fact as my shoe size. When I returned from the mountains, my mom's claim was confirmed, and some discussions followed with my boyfriend. Although there were many things we were uncertain about at that phase in our relationship, we put on a brave face and hoped for the best in supporting the gift of this child.

I was still quite numb and trying to understand how someone as dysfunctional and emotionally unstable as myself was going to care for this child in the way she rightfully deserved. I pursued various avenues of counseling and landed with enough conviction that I could somehow rise to the occasion and serve this child in a way that was far removed and superior to my own experience. For me, this meant deliberate effort and action to develop the skills I needed to be an honorable parent. I read everything available, attended counseling sessions, practiced prenatal yoga regularly, hired a doula, and continued to plan for a full-blown exodus from the ways I had learned.

I think most people who knew me were surprised by the parent I became. I was ultimately dedicated and tried to apply the latest expertise to my daughter's growth and development at every phase of her life. I restricted TV, required reading daily, homeschooled, prepared balanced and organic meals, and treated all ailments holistically. I managed play dates and arranged lessons on the violin, tennis, painting, and drama. I protected her from anything I could see coming. Although my rigorous approach to parenting came from love and was practiced with the best intentions, it turned out that my only child was living such a prescribed life that I'm not sure she ever felt a natural flow or a sense of tranquility from me. I was so caught up in ensuring she didn't experience anything similar to my childhood that I stifled my authentic self and limited what actual reality could have offered. If I had quieted my neurotic frenzy, my daughter may have been able to connect more intuitively to what she wanted and what was right for her, rather than me persistently making those assumptions.

Now a 22-year-old adult, my daughter and I are able to openly talk about my frenetic approach to parenting her and her experience as a child growing up that included little room for spontaneity. Though she eventually rebelled against my hands-on approach as a later teen, she has some good memories and seems to understand that it came from good intentions. Today, she demonstrates some tendencies of mine in the area of control, though hers are much more mild than mine were, and we can joke about it when we witness it.

Controlling parents are nothing new; we all have interacted with "helicopter parents" in various ways. Some hover in a reasonably mild way, while others exhibit controlling tendencies that border on obnoxious or fall on the spectrum of a disorder. Coming from a family pervaded with mental illness and diseases, I recognize that many people struggle with varying degrees of emotional turmoil or mental illness. I don't know what my disorder(s) may be labeled as, but I have spent my time in counseling to sort through some of the clutter to be more functional. I believe I exhibit issues with anxiety and fear of abandonment, and they have both played out consistently throughout my life. I have an extreme achievement-oriented disposition that can become quite fierce at times for those around me. Like for many who struggle with extreme dispositions or disorders, gaining control can be one of my coping mechanisms of choice.

The exertion of control can run rampant for those who feel anxious without it, particularly during unpredictable and ambiguous situations. This need for control can be destructive in personal and work relationships. Many of us who are compelled to be in control have experienced traumatic events such as abuse or neglect, which created acute feelings of vulnerability and lack of emotional or physical safety. Often this can be in the form of micromanaging others, maintaining rigid routines or diets, or maintaining cleanliness and order.

As the CEO and co-founder of a network of schools, due to my own change resistant origins of trying to control every uncomfortable situation, I devoted the first five years to either micromanaging or minimizing the effects of our staff. Due to my appetite for control, I closely monitored performance from a place of fear that my staff wasn't doing it the way I would. Anything I observed outside of my preference and comfort level was perceived as ineffective.

As our organization grew, the ability to monitor everyone's move became untenable and ineffective. With growth came increased duties and responsibilities that I could no longer handle on my own. As I looked to transition functions to others, I realized that I hadn't developed or prepared anyone adequately to take them. I had spent so much time telling them what to do and how to do it, that no one had the capacity or confidence to take them on themselves.

For the organization to survive through growth, I had to achieve the unthinkable: relinquish control. Evolving from doing everything yourself to allowing others to take on responsibilities so that you can meet overall organizational objectives is far more complicated than it sounds for a control enthusiast. For me, it became a very fluid match of give and take, and the constant discipline of letting go. Similar to developing a relationship with my grown child and allowing her to become her own person, navigate through her life, and make decisions as she sees fit, I had to encourage my key staff to do the same at work so they could find their own way to meet outcomes. Balancing empowering others while guiding their efforts, at least within certain parameters, is at first tedious, and oftentimes frustrating. As with anything else, the more you practice, the better you become at it, and the ultimate bonus is being able to watch others grow and develop before your very eyes.

The reward of witnessing others grow began to outweigh any benefits my attempts to control them ever provided. I began to not only feel more comfortable letting control go so that others could grow, I actually started to seek it out within our organization on an ongoing basis. I will note that I still have moments where the control freak will rear its ugly head, but I try to address it anytime it does begin to surface, and continue to focus on developing others not only for the sake of my overall health, but for the ultimate success of our organization. The more individuals and teams that are empowered, the more progress will be made.

Turmoil During Change

The TRACK stage of Turmoil focuses on the initial feelings of apprehension, fear of the unknown, and loss of control we may experience during change. Depending on our origins, these feelings or sensations may vary greatly in our individual responses to change. For me, the stories I've shared demonstrate my relationship with each of these feelings and the origins they stir when I experience them now during change in my life. I describe below how each of these emotions and the origins they've helped to create in me still play out in my life and influence how I interact with them as an adult and leader.

Turmoil

- Apprehension: I grew up in a home pervaded with abuse and apprehension, as we all didn't know when the next violent outburst might erupt. This has created a persistent defense mechanism in me to always be watching for where "eruptions" may take place throughout my life, and at times I falsely develop them to protect myself from potential unexpected pain or rejection. As an adult and current leader within my own organization, I have had to monitor myself closely for defaulting to this adaptation I've developed, as it can push away or confuse others when I abruptly withdraw. I pay close attention for it when I am threatened or disappointed in those reliant on me, such as my closest family or staff.

- Fear of the Unknown: Though I hold deep reactive origins with this sensation, I have managed to progress significantly with its impact in my adult life in personal and professional scenarios. A default to fear and feelings of lack of self-efficacy have been greatly resolved through years of reflection, counseling, and healing, and though the fear of certainly still comes up during volatile experiences, I can often manage it effectively. The organization I founded operates within a space of high unpredictability, which has provided me ample experience in not only developing a level of comfort with the unknown, but modeling peace with it to others.

- Loss of Control: Due to my origins mired in turmoil, I have compensated throughout my life by attempting to control as much as possible. This played out most demonstratively in my parenting, and only now that my child is an adult, have I recognized just how desperate that control was. I have spent a lot of time learning how to let go and be at peace with a lack of control in key areas in my life, especially in regard to those of whom I care for most deeply. This will be a lifelong process for me as I continue to be as aware as possible in watching for scenarios where I may attempt to grasp more control than is healthy or necessary.

Reflection

> Reflect on a specific time you may have experienced turmoil during change in your life. How did the feelings of apprehension, fear of the unknown, or discomfort play a role in your change experience? Did the feelings impact the result of the change?

Stage 2: Regret

	Stage	TRACK: Participant	
Deconstruct the Old Norm	1	Turmoil	Apprehension
			Fear of the Unknown
			Loss of Control
	2	**Regret**	**Grief**
			Disorientation
			Confusion
Construct the New Norm	3	Adjustment	Vision
			Communication
			Tenacity
	4	Commitment	Empowerment
			Individualization
			Creativity
	5	Keep	Revolutionize
			Evolve

TRACK/SHIFT Matrix

JessicaSpallino

Table 3.2 Stage 2: Regret

During the second stage of the change process, stress and anxiety transition to anguish and puzzlement. Feelings of loss, disorientation, and confusion can set in during the second stage of regret. This stage can be challenging because the security of the norm and knowing what to expect is not yet replaced with a new normal, and this can cause feelings of uneasiness and ineffectiveness.

Any change brings a sense of loss, but eventually there is a transition to something new. How we handle that transition can be critical to a successful and healthy change. The sense of loss during the change process can also reflect our past experiences with loss throughout our lives.

This stage of change ideally includes much care and guidance for ourselves and others. Patience and tolerance can be useful to allow time for personalized processes with loss, grieving, and finding new ground during an uncertain transition time.

Grief

At the age of eleven, waking up so early in the cold and dark one morning, it felt like the middle of the night. I stumbled down the hall to the barely-used formal living room, where there were a few other half-awakes sitting in the dark. My oldest brother sat on the couch in silence, my mom fidgety, across from him. I was barely coherent and unable to generate any words. To this day, I can't remember if my dad was there. Seeing his oldest of five off to the Air Force may have been more than he could have emotionally navigated, but this was a poignant event, and I also couldn't imagine him opting out of offering a Dad-style goodbye.

Just about all families have coped with the process of children growing up and leaving the nest. For my family, this was our first, and my oldest brother represented safety to me. From my perspective, Joe was a lively and entertaining grown-up whose life consisted of skateboarding, exposing us all to great music, playing guitar in a band in our garage, and always hanging out with colorful characters.

When my brother was a teenager, 70's rock music and pungent aromas emanated from the garage and throughout our home. His dynamic energy amused us all, including my dad, but oftentimes it would ignite confrontation as well. My brother's free-spirited defiance was intoxicating at times, but risky in a home with a dictator. Flare-ups would quickly transition from entertaining to tragic, depending on which end of my dad's mercurial nature presented itself.

The confrontations that resulted were always corrupted with demeaning slander and sometimes peppered with physical force. Never did they feel as though something good would come of them, nor did they create a safe place to be. Everyone in the family quickly learned to avoid confrontations as often as possible, aside from my challenging brother and then later me, when I became a defiant teen.

It could be tumultuous, but my brother created a portal to a level of excitement and hope in our home that I truly valued. I loved being around him and observing his life. My brother's departure was a tremendous loss. I held a deep sense of respect and awe for him; he seemed light and carefree even though, aside from my mom, he appeared to wrestle with much of my dad's difficulties and struggles. He characterized a safe and fun place within an often painful and intimidating environment that my dad established for us all. As the oldest, his dynamic and protective nature brought comfort to me, and I felt a lot of sadness and anxiety when he left home.

Numb and still not awake, I hugged him goodbye. I watched him drive off in the back seat of the car that dark morning and felt a sense of loss and unfamiliarity I hadn't yet experienced in my life. The adjustments that followed were anything but easy.

We have all experienced loss in our lives and will continue to do so as long as we are living. No one is immune from the experience of loss. How we cope with it may be linked to memorable experiences during formative times in our lives, creating a myriad of ways we may individually respond to something so universal.

The well-known Kübler-Ross model outlines the following five stages of grief, based on emotions experienced by terminally ill patients or those who have lost a loved one:

1. Denial

2. Anger

3. Depression
4. Bargaining
5. Acceptance

Although these stages have been frequently referenced in regard to loss, they have been equally refuted and questioned as to their demonstration, specificity, and order in which they take place. Though these five identified stages may represent common reactions to grief, responding to loss is a highly personalized process that may be quite difficult to classify with such clarity and distinctions.

Psychologists believe that denial is a natural part of our grieving process and only detrimental if we are unable to shake it. Because too much grief at once is painful to process, we naturally release grief, in smaller degrees over time, so that we may process it accordingly and in a more manageable way. The only way to truly process grief is by allowing the process to take place and working toward not abandoning your faith, others, or yourself. Although those reactions may be natural during the grieving process, it is helpful to avoid remaining in that position for too long.

Grief is a very personal process, and most often leads to acceptance. Though I was heartbroken and somewhat lost when my brother left, I eventually accepted it, adjusted, and carried on with life and the new normal. We almost all finally accept and move on after we experience loss, and we transition to the new way of life. Any change that we are presented with involves the loss of something and the addition of something new. The way we go through the process is highly individualized. In accommodating others' processes with loss, it is essential to remember that what may work for one person may not work at all for another.

The organization I co-founded has been built on continuous change. Due to a temperamental industry pervaded with perpetual legislative changes and proposed barriers from competitors, we've had to manage a variety of responses to an ever-evolving industry. We've gone through significant modifications to our fundamental model several times, and throughout the past several years we built our own technological systems while we were in the process of using them.

Our team members' responses to the continuously changing environment have been as varied as the changes themselves. Every change adopter has been represented within our organization. The defiants simply weren't interested in working within an inconsistent model and left, while the resistors felt anxious and needed to complain about it publicly or privately. The supporters just put their heads down, did their work, and tried to keep up, and the implementors invested in the change and worked to contribute to ongoing solutions.

While none of the individuals within the aforementioned groups were necessarily wrong for how they responded to changes, I think it's safe to say which ones employers prefer. I ultimately value people who contribute to ongoing solutions during changes, especially in a change-fluid organization. These groups will be referred to again in Chapter 5, but the point here is that everyone handles loss differently. If that reality isn't considered during any change, it can create major challenges within a professional setting, and certainly personally as well.

Losing a parent is unfortunate, but it is an expected part of adult life. The loss of my parents marked a very pivotal time in my life. My mom died suddenly of a heart attack at 69 years old. I talked to her on a Thursday, and she was healthy and pleasant as ever, and she was gone the following Monday morning. She suffered a heart attack in a casino hotel room with my dad in the High Desert, and they waited too long to call 911.

After an inconsistent relationship with my dad as an adult, my brothers and sisters and I had to work diligently to maintain some sort of relationship with him after my mom's death. We managed to stay in contact with him for several months, but he eventually diverted to his usual cycle of complete alienation and isolation and couldn't be reached. I was on my way to a business meeting when I received a call from my sister. My dad's neighbors had sensed something was wrong when they hadn't seen him for over a week, and the smell of gas was permeating his California High Desert neighborhood.

My sister was the first to his house. He had created a contraption to emit gas within the house, and he was found dead in his closet with his dog, still alive, lying on his chest. My mom's ashes were cupped in his arm. There was no official note, but there were clues that it was something he was planning to do, and it was likely put into action on his birthday. At the time of his death, none of us had spoken to him for over a year.

My siblings and I united, as we did when my mom passed, to support each other and sort all of the details. We all were struggling with it in varying ways; some of us were numb, and others were utterly wrecked. My dad had spent the last year of his life entirely alone, likely grappling with his untreated illness and disorders. The powerlessness we all felt deeply impacted each of us during our grieving process, creating uncertain paths ahead of us.

I know that most adults lose their parents at some point in their lives, mourn the loss, and move on with their lives in a healthy, functional manner. My reaction to the loss of both my mom and especially my dad was anything but healthy or functional. After my dad died as tragically as he did, I felt as though I not only lost both of my parents but also trust and understanding of life itself, along with any last hope that my foundation as a person was secure. I'd imagine this could be considered part of an initial phase of grieving, but what followed was the unraveling of my life as I knew it. My brothers and sisters all handled this loss in their ways, and even today, many years later, we all still react to the loss in our own unique manners. Over time, I experienced a complete overhaul of both my personal and professional life, and the loss of my parents was the ultimate catalyst.

As I experience loss throughout my life, it often feels as it did that early morning when my brother left a noticeable absence in our home. Losing your parents and watching your older siblings grow and move on with their adult lives is often a fundamentally natural process. My process with this type of loss, such as that of my parents, carried a lot of weight and potential dysfunction based on my past experiences. When you think of change, imagine everyone in the world and the lens that was created by their personal experiences. In doing so, it's easy to see how complex change becomes when we consider the infinite perspectives people have in response to the feelings of loss that change can evoke. This consideration may impact how we implement change.

Disorientation

I had many friends growing up and throughout high school, but I had a specific group of friends with whom I trudged through the years. Most of us were typical teens, engaging in trouble and shenanigans on occasion. We could be a little wild, and for me, the wildness started around the time I turned 13. I was overanxious and undersupported, and therefore my teen years were a recipe for disaster.

Like every other teenager stumbling through those disorienting years, I fought through with a little extra carelessness, leaving wreckage at nearly every turn. During this time of increased peer pressure and identity formation, I mostly felt like an aimless wanderer with no grounding. I didn't know who I was or where I was headed, and I was terrified to find out. I fabricated an identity to be accepted amongst my popular peers, but I often felt like an imposter. I believed that the authentic me wasn't even close to acceptable, and it scared me immensely. In order to cope, I sought out destructive ways to medicate and numb the pain, despair, and anxiety. I abused substances that would enable me to completely check out and not have to continue to feel the angst.

My friends grew tired of taking care of me when we went out. I developed a dangerous habit of seeking isolation once medicated, and I would often find myself in precarious situations, either discovered by strangers or the police. My parents weren't necessarily available or reachable during these times, since they would go to bed early each evening and never answered the home phone. My poor brother, who was just a few years older, but far more coherent and together than I was, would often be forced into recovering and saving me. Like my sister, who had been overburdened by the responsibility to oversee me, my brother was in the unfair position as the one who had to continuously bail me out of trouble. On one occasion when he came to recover me, a police officer gave him his card, and expressed his concern, offering to connect me to resources that could help. At the time, neither my brother nor I had the capacity to take him up on it.

During this time, I felt utterly lost with nowhere to turn. My parents were neither physically nor emotionally available. My being in constant trouble put a strain on my siblings who were often forced to handle me, and based on my erratic and destructive behavior, I was in the process of destroying all peer relationships. I can remember when my problems started, in a cry for help I went to my mom to tell her, and she replied, "There are some things I just don't want to know." Looking back, I know my mom was trying to survive her own existence in a volatile setting, but as a 13-year-old starting to lose myself to a variety of dangerous and destructive habits, I took the lack of investment as confirmation that there was no one there to support and help me. I had no direction or peace due to a constant feeling of unrest and despair. The more I acted out, the worse I felt.

Whether the change is voluntary or involuntary, it can be a process to adjust. The teen years are one of the most unstable developmental times in our lives, wavering on a continuously dynamic foundation and bringing about physiological, emotional, hormonal, and social changes—sometimes daily. The way we respond to this volatile period depends on a variety of factors, including our capacity for change and the unknown.

My teen years brought a lot of danger and destruction because I could not cope with the transient nature of the time and found the only way to cope was to not deal with it at all. The anxiety I felt created such disorientation that I was unable to be a rational participant in my life. As I look back on these days, I am not sure how I made it out of that period alive.

Anxiety disorientation can plague us in different forms and varying levels of severity during times of extreme stress and angst. Fundamental disorientation can impair the ability to focus on the present and anything taking place during the current moment. Thoughts may be challenging to follow, and one may have the feeling of being trapped in a cycle of their own thoughts. In extreme situations, anxiety and disorientation can escalate. A person may experience rapid thoughts and hyperventilation, which are common symptoms of a panic attack. These racing thoughts consume an individual with feelings and symptoms that there is an inability to focus on anything else.

My daughter was sixteen years old when I left the home where we raised her. Throughout my life, I never imagined I would marry, as I instinctively knew I wasn't equipped for it. Later in my life, I came to believe I would never be capable of going through with a divorce.

Out of respect for my family's privacy, I won't get into the complications within my marriage, but the period just before and after our divorce marks the darkest time in my life. Upon our separation, I moved to an apartment nearby, and my daughter spent her senior year transporting herself between the house and the apartment. She began demonstrating volatile teen behavior after her grandpa's death and the divorce. I always thought I would avoid the wild and rebellious teenage stage with her, since she didn't experience the emotional abuse and mental illness I had growing up. I was gravely mistaken.

After she graduated from high school she left for Utah to begin college, but the transition was far too soon and extreme for her. She hadn't been given the time or support to deal with the divorce. Between her departure and return home within a year, I had moved from the apartment to my sister's for a little while, and then again to another apartment located in between two of my organization's sites, thinking it would be more convenient.

I had lost both parents, my marriage, the home I had been living in for nearly 20 years, my pets, most of my belongings, and about all of the friendships I had developed during my daughter's childhood. My daughter had since come back from Utah and moved in with her boyfriend. There wasn't a single familiar thing left in my life other than my job and the two year old organization I had built with my co-founder.

I felt like a complete failure to my daughter and myself, and the guilt of divorce was consuming me. I felt responsible for all the pain and dysfunction my daughter experienced and questioned myself as a person. I became so lonely and lost that I sank in a deep, disorienting depression. There were several dark days and nights that I had very real suicidal thoughts. As I thought of ways that I could end my misery, I thought of my daughter every time and knew that it was something I just couldn't do to her. Somehow, I dragged myself through each day.

Later, I moved to a rental house close to one of my organization's sites. I felt a bit more comfortable. I had a lot more space, a yard to get out in, and I was five minutes from my work. I began to progress through the dark depression, but there were days that I felt so alone. I would work outside in the yard every weekend as my dad used to do, and I felt this dark cloud hanging over my head. I was afraid that I was destined to end up like him — deceased, in my house alone, and nobody would even notice I was gone. My dad's ghost and the way he ended his life was something I had to get comfortable with. I had to recognize that although I may have some similarities to him, it didn't necessarily mean that my life was predetermined for me.

The overload of loss and change brought me to one of the most significant breaking points of my adult life. Change overload can do this to us, just as it did to my daughter during the overload of change and loss she had to face in her life. Allowing time and support during these periods can be critical not only for our peace, but in extreme cases, for our survival.

Confusion

My middle school years brought ample opportunities to escape from my sometimes-trying life at home. I managed to develop an array of friendships with many highly gregarious classmates, and became a part of a somewhat-active social network.

Almost every weekend I was at a friend's house enjoying sleepovers, partaking in various activities, or even joining in on an array of family vacations with friends and their families. This diversification to my social life changed the constitution and pains of daily life. Multifarious experiences and personalities suddenly stimulated me. In turn, I was able to investigate just how similar and yet very different my home life was from my friends'.

There was one particular friend whose life exemplified the antithesis of mine in all respects. She lived in the most upscale neighborhood in a large, beautiful home with a resort-style backyard with a pool. She had the most beautiful things, dressed impeccably, and always looked like she just stepped off a magazine photo shoot. She was part of a divorced family, which I had never experienced, and she'd often quietly express that there was some turmoil between her stepdad and stepbrothers and sisters. She was very kind, and never came across as pretentious. Her mom made sure she invited friends over regularly.

I spent many weekends at her house and joined her family on many vacations. One evening when I was visiting their home, I felt incredibly out of place. When I walked downstairs to go out to dinner with her family, her mother asked me to change my clothes. Coming from a strictly blue-collar, working-class home, we believed that needing to be dressed up for a casual dinner outing was contrived and pretentious. As a family of seven living on my dad's lineman salary, we had always lived modestly, and had very little beyond the necessities. We maintained a strict alignment with the viewpoint of the underdog and minority. If my dad ever won it big at the racetrack, and we found ourselves in a restaurant such as one I'd visit with my friend, I imagine our troop might have stood out. I was trained to be very compliant, so though I was embarrassed and confused by the focus on want I viewed as quite trivial, I happily changed into something of my friends to wear as instructed by her mom.

I'd often feel judgmental and ungracious upon returning home after a stay at this friend's house. I'd be genuinely upset that we didn't have an enormous swimming pool with a cascading waterfall, or organic avocado cream stocked in the bathroom for post hand washings.

I lost touch with my close friend once we started high school, since we were assigned to different high schools. Shockingly, during the first couple of years of high school, she killed herself in the very same room we used to create scrapbooks and share innocent laughs. This change left me incredibly confused and desperately grasping for anything that could help me make sense of her decision to take her own life. I tried to imagine the pain and desperation she must have been feeling to consider that as an option and the devastation to her family. Up until this experience, I had never felt such confusion over a loss, and it opened my eyes to just how complex each of our lives and experiences are. We can never truly know what people are going through no matter how much we may think we do, and this requires us to be even more tolerant and patient with each person's process. Much later in my life, I felt this same confusion and pain when my dad took his life. Any loss can be quite devastating and even more so when loved ones decide to leave us at their own will.

Sudden and unexpected change can create confusion as to how to make sense of and adjust to the modified reality. When one struggles with justifying or making sense of the change, it can be tough to move forward with it constructively. I'm sure we have all witnessed or heard of a scenario where someone just isn't the same after a traumatic or unexplainable change. This can often be when those faced with overwhelming confusion over a loss or change turn to religious or spiritual beliefs to help make sense of it and find some level of acceptance and peace to move forward in their lives. We all have likely turned to something ethereal to get us through extremely challenging times.

I am writing this chapter during the unprecedented COVID-19 pandemic. At this time, we have been practicing social distancing for nearly eight months, with most schools still closed and many businesses trying to hold on considering the impact. Just about everything has gone online and the president of the United States and many of the White House staff have contracted the virus. Much is uncertain as we wait for a vaccine that may bring some relief, but life as we knew it is almost nonexistent.

This worldwide pandemic has created a new reality we never thought we would witness outside of a fictional disaster movie. For most people, the lifestyle we have been accustomed to has been replaced with complete disorientation and confusion. Getting into a supermarket has become an ordeal—some only allow ten people in at a time, with masks required, and a strict maintenance of six feet between yourself and anyone else. As we've grown accustomed to the new norm, many people are worried about the unknown future, grieving over the loss of "normal" life, and feeling confused about how to carry on with our lives with direction, purpose, and comfort.

My organization had been operating entirely online for nearly two years when the pandemic broke out, so we've been very fortunate not to have to modify our practices and still serve our students effectively throughout the crisis. Our teachers and staff have been hardworking and dedicated well beyond basic expectations. However, I made a mistake in thinking that since we weren't that impacted operationally, and most employees were grateful to be stable and securely employed during such a tumultuous time, that all was well.

Although we accelerated our support and the services available to our staff and families, the level of demoralization that many of them felt created a dull and strained climate. It had become clear that many of our staff needed additional support, time to cope, and tolerance for variation in practices and daily schedules. The confusion about the state of the world and the future began to wear them down, and care was needed to deal with all the loss and uncertainty.

Times of deep confusion like this, when people are experiencing loss and disorientation, can require many to look for meaning to stay on a purposeful path. Often, we turn to our religious or spiritual beliefs during these times to make sense of such perplexing events. Many fall back on key support relationships, or even practices such as exercising, spending time on hobbies, or being outdoors to help ease the strain of confusion. We are all more at peace when we feel a sense of purpose with clarity in our lives.

I've tried writing this book several times throughout the years and couldn't find the inspiration to complete it until I applied it to my own life and personal stories. Once I was able to understand my attraction to the topic, based on my own experiences, I felt a real calling to share with others in hopes it may help them with change challenges in their lives. When that became more and more clear, the book just wrote itself.

Regret During Change

Regret is the second stage of TRACK and deals with the deeply impactful feelings of grief, disorientation and confusion we experience during change. As with any other TRACK stage, individual responses may differ based on origins of the participant and my personal stories reflect some of my own. Below is a brief description of each stage and their influence on my personal and professional life.

Regret

- Grief: No one is immune from experiencing loss, and therefore grief. From losing a way we've always done things at work to losing a close loved one, everyone's grieving process may differ. My experience with grief as a change participant from a personal perspective is one that is deeply emotional and often requires significant alone time to sort my feelings and heal. From a professional perspective, I tend to welcome change and shedding old ways of doing things, though that is not the case with all those I manage. This is an ongoing challenge within my organization and ensuring that change implementations are amply supported is a key focus. Supporting the varying change adopter categories is a challenge I continue to work at and learn from.

- Disorientation: Those with mild resistant origins to change may feel less disorientation during change. Within my organization there are staff members that, thrive during change and they almost seem stimulated by it. They revert to problem solving and genuinely see the possibility generated from the change. There are others, however, who exhibit extreme strain and tend to view change as something they would like to halt. This is where I lean on my own origins, versed in change, to continue to support others during the change and find a balance that all can be comfortable with and support.

- Confusion: I have found that confusion can often be a symptom of change when there is not enough information or planning involved to guide all participants.

This is where ample planning, guidance, and communication are critical. Within my organization, we have made a concerted effort to enhance our updates and directives to ensure that staff who feel confused are regularly informed and assessed to identify where there are gaps in communication. Beyond the planning, however, confusion can also be caused by the stress that change creates for those with change fatigue. Understanding the vision and the purpose of the change can help participants and leaders with a guiding reminder of why the change is taking place.

Reflection

> Recall any personal stories of your own where you may have experienced regret during change or loss in your life. How did the feelings of grief, disorientation, or confusion appear in your change experience? Did the feelings impact the change process in your life?

Chapter 4: Phase 2: Constructing the Norm

The last three stages of change represent the process of constructing a new norm upon the change. Modeling and delivering the means to implement the change is crucial during this phase to empower those to transition to the new norm. As with any construction, building a strong foundation is essential for transformation to be possible, along with close attention to strong origins during these stages.

Stage 3: Adjustment

TRACK/SHIFT Matrix			
	Stage	**TRACK: Participant**	
Deconstruct the Old Norm	1	Turmoil	Apprehension
			Fear of the Unknown
			Loss of Control
	2	Regret	Grief
			Disorientation
			Confusion
Construct the New Norm	3	Adjustment	Vision
			Communication
			Tenacity
	4	Commitment	Empowerment
			Individualization
			Creativity
	5	Keep	Revolutionize
			Evolve

JessicaSpallino

Table 4.1 Stage 3: Adjustment

The next stage of change is the most pivotal of them all. The first stages of Turmoil and Grief reflect deep resistance or disorientation from the change, and most of our energy is devoted to either resisting the change or trying to make any sense of it. The adjustment stage demonstrates a shift from resistance and turmoil, to a level of acceptance and engagement in taking initial steps to support the change.

Developing a vision for the change, communicating that vision, and exhibiting the tenacity to see it through are all critical for the change to be active and sustainable. As we walk through these three steps, we'll take a look at where our capacity for them may lie and how we can call upon our origins to see through change.

Vision

My screams became muffled as I wedged as much of my six-year-old body as I could under the driver seat of our white Ford Hornet. It was my first time at a drive-in movie theatre, and it was an experience I'd never forget. Like most other family movie experiences, this revolved around the latest terrifying horror movie, *The Omen*. I had no idea what the movie was about—I just knew that I didn't like it, and I wanted it to stop. To survive it, I tried crawling under the car seat, where my younger brother joined me for safety. Family movie outings usually included all seven family members, and we had seen all the latest horror movies: *Phantasm*, *The Exorcist*, *The Fog*, *It's Alive*, and many others, whether we liked it or not.

For my ninth birthday, my dad treated my good friend, Kim, and I to a dinner at Tastee-Freez and then to a light movie called *Midnight Express*, which is about a young American caught by Turkish police while attempting to smuggle hashish out of Istanbul. He lands in prison for four years, where he endures violent and graphic abuse and learns that the Turkish High Court has added 30 years to his sentence. He becomes demoralized and determines that his only option is to attempt to escape. Kim and I kept our hands over our eyes for the majority of the movie and felt relieved once it was over. We didn't understand most of the content, but our young instincts were honed enough to tell us it was dark, intense, and beyond what we could process. Later the following week, Kim didn't act the same when I saw her at school. When I asked her if she wanted to come over, she confessed that she wasn't allowed to go to my house anymore due to the traumatic R-rated movie experience.

Looking back, I believe that I combatted growing up with exposure to dark and scary subject matter by seeking out fantasies with wholesome and virtuous storylines. I turned to *Little House on the Prairie* regularly to appease my craving for a safe, traditional, and structured family life. Though I loved my parents and saw much good in them, I also recognized things were more volatile than they were supposed to be. I found solace in the relationship between Laura Ingalls and Pa. I identified with how the rough and tumble Laura often compared herself to her softer and prettier sister, and how Pa always accepted and cared for her regardless of her human flaws. When I watched *Little House on the Prairie*, I felt as though paternal nirvana was possible, no matter how imperfect we all may be.

I've realized I spent most of my childhood envisioning an ideal family life, with more available and nurturing parents. I can't imagine I am the only person who has wished their parents were better equipped for the job of parenting, but I think I survived some of the painful parts of my childhood by transferring my yearning for a more conventional home with a vision of what it could and should be.

I can remember often feeling so troubled by the lack of attention and care that I needed but felt unmet. I would often turn to my sister to comfort me or even take on a more mothering role, which was destined to fail, as we both were just trying to get by in an environment that wasn't very nurturing, I slowly learned to rely on myself and any connections I could make in the world that would help me get by. When I was six-years-old, I inherited a pair of roller skates from my cousin and was intrigued to learn how to use them. I remember harassing other people to teach me how to use them, but soon realized that if I wanted to skate it would be solely up to me to figure it out. One sunny Saturday morning, I laced up and began trying to roller skate in our backyard. The more I tried, the more I saw myself as an experienced roller skater. I became so obsessed with this vision that I stayed out there until the sun was setting. Covered with scrapes and bruises, my mom finally ordered me inside, and I went to sleep that night with one of the most memorable moments of my childhood: if you want something, you're going to have to make it happen on your own, and you can't give up. Maybe we've all experienced a similarly empowering moment at some time throughout our lives. For me, it was one I'll never forget.

Though I had developed some coping mechanisms to deal with the deficiencies throughout my childhood, I became emotionally impaired, and during my teen years I completely rebelled and checked out. The years that followed were a rollercoaster of bad choices and consistent destructive actions because I had no vision for who I could be and where I wanted to go.

During this time of the COVID-19 pandemic, many K-12 schools continue to struggle with facilitating online learning for their students. Most traditional seat-based schools have turned to online learning for now, in hopes to reopen soon. Some schools, like my own, have utilized online or blended learning as the core modality since its inception. These schools have had to make minimal modifications to their programs, while others have struggled to adapt in such a short time. Many schools, including my own, have experienced a surge in enrollments for those families looking for programs more experienced in online learning in order to get the needed support in a modality unfamiliar to them.

Working in this unique educational space for so many years has put my organization in a position to develop our own online tools and curriculum to use as a key aspect of our educational program. During this challenging time for schools, my organization has provided free use of our tools and curriculum in hopes of offering support to those schools not native to online learning, yet we've received only a couple of takers. There are probably a variety of reasons, but I think the most likely is the lack of vision these schools have to guide their transition to a different learning modality. Schools and districts have been forced to scramble to conduct a complete overhaul of their model almost overnight. The usual stages of change, fear of the unknown, loss of control, and grief have all been abruptly merged into the one, without time for any of them to process or permeate norms or expectations sufficiently. Developing a vision for how things may look moving forward can be challenging to accomplish in such a short amount of time and while they are still fielding struggling families.

Revolutionary or evolutionary change is disruptive and most successful with time to accommodate the stages throughout the change. Developing a vision for change is critical for the change to be successful and to support others through the process. It is so much easier to sustain and invest in change when we can see what it will look like and how impactful it will be.

Communication

I had never sat with someone, formally talking one on one, focusing only on my feelings and experiences. I left the first several sessions sweating and wondering what difference it was going to make. At the time I started counseling, I was a full-time college student and waitressing full-time to support myself. I had found myself in so many empty relationships that I intuitively knew it was time to do something.

I was unclear of the impact in the beginning, but I believe my trust and relationship with my therapist, was what kept me showing up. I found myself intrigued by the process of unraveling my life history and making meaning behind critical events, relationships, and experiences. I found my counselor to be funny, caring, and warmly blunt. Her sense of humor was real and surprisingly down to earth, considering her upper-class status and privileged position. Her honest sense of the world made me feel safe and comforted, but it was anything but sugarcoated. It was real.

We examined the initial reason that prompted me to try counseling, which was yet another unsavory character I chose to be in a relationship with. This one decided to pursue my roommate while I was away at work, and my poor roommate didn't know how to tell me. Finally having a place to talk deeply about my life and ongoing turmoil was refreshing, and it was something I needed at the time. Communicating honestly and vulnerably was something I had never done before, and it seemed to free me of what felt like deep, dark secrets I had been holding onto.

I began to see some changes in myself and started to feel a slight sense of peace, which I had never felt before. I committed to continuing the sessions while I waitressed full-time and carried a full course load in college. My life became all work, and I didn't mind it. It took a couple of years to uncover the many scars and tendencies that were keeping me from finding peace and purpose. Once many of those were identified and somewhat understood, it was meaningless if I couldn't forgive and move on to my own life. I had struggled with resentment toward many people that I figured should have provided a particular environment that was safe and nurturing. Counseling helped me to better understand why I still battled with the anger and feelings of inadequacy that not receiving it created.

Communication within my organization has undoubtedly been vital in general, but it is invaluable during change efforts. As an organization anchored in its vision, yet fluid in its development, the culture in which we work is one of continuous change. At the time of our organization's inception, the independent study charter space was oversaturated. In the beginning, we were bringing in fewer enrollments than we anticipated, so we opened our doors trying to please anyone who expressed an interest, even if they weren't a natural fit for our model.

This created an impossible situation for the entire community. In a desperate attempt to stay in business, we detoured from our original plan to operate primarily as an independent study model with the site available for student and teacher meetings and to only hold supplemental classes and activities. Instead, based on parent feedback, we transitioned to a four day a week on-site program. This transition resulted in many issues, as we weren't necessarily built for all of our students to be enrolled on-site at the same time. It created issues that were as small as seating arrangements, to bigger issues such as student behaviors and the ability for students to focus well on their academics. Thinking back to this time still makes me a little nauseous, but it has been an incredible learning experience, and it is one I will always call upon. We lost some employees and students, partially due to a lack of initial enrollments, but mostly due to a misalignment to our original vision and chaotic communication to all impacted stakeholders. Looking back, we could have regularly communicated the issues we were having for real transparency, addressed the challenges, and worked together to come up with solutions. We may still have lost some employees and families, but we would have been far better off if we had employed a thorough and systematic communication process during such a tumultuous time.

Six years later, after many painful lessons learned, and with the organization stable and successful, I send out an all-staff survey quarterly to get candid feedback on how the organization is doing in a variety of areas, including leadership, support, training, and everything in between. Two main issues emerged from the staff. The first issue was communication. After established annual objectives and key results and what felt like endless meetings and messaging tools deployed, staff expressed a need for improvement in general communication. And to further this feedback, they expressed a need for improvement in communication during times of change.

Although this may not be the most shocking feedback for a very dynamic organization, it was surprising, since our leadership team devoted a significant portion of their time communicating to their teams. Yet, we still found that it wasn't enough. I believe this is due to the value of keeping others apprised of developments and confirming their participation in the solution discussions. Ensuring that communication regarding change is delivered before the change takes place can help with change fatigue. We run into technological issues on an ongoing basis while building our own systems, and are often required to make changes to the system we hadn't necessarily planned for. When this happens it creates frustration for our staff, so we have further developed a variety of communication tools and systems to ensure that staff knows of the change as soon as it has taken place. As we continue to grow, effective communication across departments and multiple projects is essential if we wish to maintain a supportive and professional environment where everyone's contributions feel valued and impactful.

I usually watch the news while I ran on the treadmill each morning. There were usually political stories with other news sprinkled in. Now, it is solely COVID-19 pandemic updates around the clock from various places throughout the country. In an effort to inform and comfort citizens of this country, each state holds press conferences regularly, often daily. This ongoing communication attempts to minimize the uncertainty and angst many are feeling during these unprecedented times. For every concern one may have, there is a message to address it and provide some level of control during a time when little control over the situation is felt.

Tenacity

When the seven of us piled into the 1971 AMC Hornet, it usually meant good-spirited fun and what we would have considered good family time. Family outings were strictly limited to the beach, Disneyland, horse races, or to eat out. This Saturday felt slightly different as we launched the overloaded sedan onto the freeway, because the full details of the outing were not shared with us.

Once we got off the freeway, I assumed we were headed to the horse races, since we were in that neighborhood. Instead, we pulled into a parking lot that led to several tennis courts. We had never played tennis or any other sport together, so even though the destination was finally revealed, we were even more confused than before. My dad ordered us to all get out of the car while he grabbed some things out of the trunk, including five or six big, handled buckets.

Well-trained, we obediently vacated the car and tentatively waited for instructions. My dad handed us each a bucket and an assigned area along the ivy-covered slopes that encompassed the courts. The small army of laborers was then released to their units to recover as many forever lost tennis balls fouled by local tennis players as possible. We were accustomed to doing exactly what we were told, and once the bewilderment of the mission wore off, we disbursed to our stations.

The innate achiever in me was thrilled by the assignment, and even though I had no idea what we needed tennis balls for, with complete and total purpose, I grasped onto the ivy branches to pull myself up the hillsides. I developed a tennis ball search and rescue strategy that involved gripping tightly onto a primary vine conduit with one hand while using the other to pillage through the bushes to locate the hidden balls.

The fluorescent yellow balls began to appear nestled within the ivy cover ground like discovered gold sparkling amongst the bland earth. The more tennis balls I found, the more motivated I became to fill my bucket. Once I exhausted the first uphill climb, I wandered, within as well as beyond my assigned area, to find more.

During a brief lull, I noticed that my bucket was about half full. Sweaty and dirty, I looked around to see what progress my competition had made. Other buckets were almost full; I scurried on to another section to be sure I returned with sufficient findings. Upon return with a full bucket, my dad surveyed our treasure and showed moderate satisfaction, which was enough to appease the team of approval seekers. We piled back in the car, trunk full of used tennis balls, and devoured our usual shared meals at our favorite Mexican restaurant.

I imagine I view tennis balls differently than most due to this experience, and this is one will stay with me forever. To this day, I am not sure what we did with all of the tennis balls that we gathered, other than play with some of them as kids, while the rest likely sat in buckets in the garage. Looking back, it was probably part of my dad's compulsion to "win" something, like he did at the horse races or in the stuffed animal claw machines. As unusual as it may be, it is one that conjured up my origins in tenacity—or grit, if you prefer—that I find has been critical in navigating any change or challenge in my life. Due to my tenacious origins, I have a hard time accepting that I am not able to achieve anything to which I set my mind. My tenacity can backfire on occasion, and I find myself feeling like I'm in over my head.

My love for music landed me in a position that I single-handedly pursued—to sing at my brother's wedding. My daughter was about five months old when I began to prepare for the performance. I selected the song, recruited my oldest and extremely-seasoned musician brother to play the guitar, and practiced as often as I could between changing diapers and bartending. The big event was on a typically hot June day, and I was far more nervous than I expected. I couldn't shake the feeling that if I blew it, it would forever tarnish the most important day of my brother's wedded future. My oldest brother, cool as a cucumber, played as beautifully as ever, and I sang to the best of my rehearsed ability. As I looked out into the crowd, I watched my five-year-old niece, seated next to my sister, covering her ears. Today, I still joke with my niece that her candid feedback saved me from a lifetime of disappointment trying to become a famous singer.

I eventually came to terms with the fact that I wasn't destined to sing professionally or become a rock star. Although I may have fallen short as a wedding-singer, I realized that day that even though we may not always land exactly where we want to with our efforts, it's very often the grit we learn and grow from that has the most impact on our life's trajectory. Committing to endeavors that we are uncomfortable with condition us in humility and stamina, which are valuable in weathering change. This can develop that muscle of tenaciousness that is required when plowing through real and meaningful change. I just hope my brother and his wife don't forever hold the opportunity for my personal growth against me.

Tenacity developed into pure grit has served the organization I cofounded quite well. It would have dissolved years ago without it. The volatile space in which charter schools operate requires constant pivoting and modifications to the program based on ongoing established regulations. Because charter schools are newer within the educational arena and initially treated as a purely alternative option, the growth in interest and enrollments have caused tighter rules in an attempt to better monitor them. However, some believe the rules are strictly instituted to stifle their growth due to the competition they present within the market.

As with any new business, the first couple of years of the organization were anything but stable and smooth. We had legitimate concerns regarding the disconnect between the problems in the market and how we thought we were solving them. Our original model offered elements that the market didn't necessarily want, and it was impacting our ability to stay in business. We were always worried about covering costs and maintaining our survival.

Things came to a head during our second year of operation, when our authorizer called us to meet. We were not meeting our enrollment projections, and we had an understated cash position on our end of year budget report that didn't reflect state awarded funds. They were ready to close us down. We knew we had some work to do to get where we needed to be, but we didn't realize just how close we were to losing everything. I remember sitting in the meeting, thinking I had failed and was in completely over my head. I represented the educational program and product side of the organization, while my co-founder's experience was on the business and marketing side, so while I was the CEO and I usually led the conversation, I desperately deferred to him.

As he explained all of the factors at play and any inaccuracies they were presented with, I sat there and realized just how deep we were going to need to dig to recover. We had developed a plan to share with them to address any shortfalls. Yet again, I accessed that young, tenacious girl scrambling for tennis balls as if my life depended on it, not only to get through this challenge but ultimately to change the way we did business. We developed a plan that convinced our authorizer we would recover from the shortfall and eventually thrive as an organization. They agreed to allow us the time to acquire the growth we needed.

We left the meeting with an uphill battle ahead of us, but we each defaulted to our intrinsic nature of working our way through the problem and never giving up. From that day forward, we remained laser-focused on growing our enrollment by solving a unique challenge in our specific educational space, which was providing a rigorous and accountable summer school program with efficient delivery systems. Utilizing my co-founder's business and system building skills along with my sales background, we were able to completely turn our organization around and scale it to a level that not only caught us up but put us ahead. Our authorizers were pleased, and our success was celebrated.

Once we overcame this initial shortfall hurdle, additional regulations came to light for charter schools based on a lack of clear expectations, and some unethical charter school leaders—the exact program we were being celebrated for—suddenly became a target for interrogation. Some school districts are not in support of charter schools due to the new competition they bring to the educational market and enrollments they may lose to charter schools. When an unethical charter school leader committed fraud and stole over $50 million in the biggest scandal in charter school history, every other charter school was left looking like they might be unethical as well. Yet again, we had to lean on our gritty and tenacious origins to prove who we were, what we stood for, and that we were not only on the right side of things, but committed to becoming a true leader in our space. Without our tenacity, our organization would have never survived.

Adjustment During Change

The TRACK stage of Adjustment centers on the concepts of vision, communication, and tenacity we may experience during change. Depending on our origins, these feelings or sensations may vary greatly in our individual responses to change. For me, the stories I've shared demonstrate my relationship with each of these feelings and the origins they stir when I experience them now during change in my life. I've described below how each of these emotions and the origins they've helped to create in me still play out in my life and how I interact with them as an adult and leader.

Adjustment

- Vision: The need to develop a vision for anything new or unprecedented is universal and has been a tool I have relied on many times throughout my life when I have struggled during change and needed guidance. I have utilized the power of vision during tough times growing up and certainly through transitional periods in my personal life. Within my organization, I have found the vision for any change to be critical, that it should be the first thing to develop in order to construct the new norm. During a change within my organization from on-site instruction to complete online instruction, staff had a difficult time understanding how it would work and how effective it may be. In fact, two defiants left the organization when we made the decision to transition to online only. I found that once we were able to create a vision for what it would like and how we'd empower the teachers to be effective, were they able to become change supporters and implementors to support the change.

- Communication: Ensuring that communication is consistent during change is crucial to ensure the change participants are empowered with information and know what to expect. Communication with implementors and supporters keeps the change moving along and maintains communication with the resistors and defiants, which is key in evaluating how serious their resistance may be. I've been at an organization where communication wasn't consistent. This can leave the resistors and defiants free to not only make their own assumptions about the change, but to share those assumptions with others, potentially transitioning supporters and implementors to their way of oppositional thinking. When in doubt, overcommunicate during change.

- Tenacity: There isn't a single leadership scenario shared in this book that doesn't demonstrate the utmost tenacity in seeing through a change. There will always be reasons for a potential change to not take place. Not the right time, not enough resources, etc. If you have evaluated the need for the change and you believe in it wholeheartedly, then it will require an appetite for tenaciousness to ensure the change comes to fruition. Like with any change, there will always be resistance and it will need to be met with the tenacity to see it through. I have found tenacity to be essential in any change within my organization, and have often had to rely on the tenacity of change implementors and supporters within my organization to help see it through.

Reflection

> Think of a specific time you have had to make uncomfortable adjustments as part of a change in your life. How did relying on a vision, communication, and the need for tenacity impact your change experience? Did any of these aspects come easier than others? Why or why not?

Stage 4: Commitment

The Commitment stage of the change process involves fortifying the change effort by utilizing empowerment, individualization, and creativity. While many of the other stages may deal with our inherent nature and potential resistant tendencies, this one involves reaching out to others and nurturing their personal investment in the change.

	Stage	TRACK: Participant	
TRACK/SHIFT Matrix			
Deconstruct the Old Norm	1	Turmoil	Apprehension
			Fear of the Unknown
			Loss of Control
	2	Regret	Grief
			Disorientation
			Confusion
Construct the New Norm	3	Adjustment	Vision
			Communication
			Tenacity
	4	Commitment	**Empowerment**
			Individualization
			Creativity
	5	Keep	Revolutionize
			Evolve

JessicaSpallino

Table 4.2 Stage 4: Commitment

Even if those impacted by the change have come to terms with it and have begun to embrace the vision, if they do not continue to invest in it at this stage, the change very often loses momentum and doesn't come to fruition. Empowering others in individualized and creative ways is what helps change efforts gain strength and persist to the last stage of transformation, where change is likely to be successful and sustainable.

Empowerment

I hadn't realized I was speeding until I saw the old police car behind me, lights flashing. As I pulled to the side of the deserted road, dust enveloped my burgundy rental car. The officer looked like he was straight out of a movie. He was dressed in a southwestern uniform, unlike any I had seen in Southern California, pointed hat and all. He might have even had a toothpick hanging to a side of his mouth, or maybe I imagined that part. For a second, I realized that I might be vulnerable on the deserted highway, not another car or person was in sight; I was 24 years old and traveling alone. Our exchange was dedicated to the benefits of driving the speed limit, and after his brief lecture, he let me go on my way.

My solo road trip was to be about eight nights throughout the Southwest. I hadn't made a single hotel reservation, because I was 24 and figured I'd find appropriate lodgings as I went. I brought enough cash with me to cover hotel rooms, food, and gas. We didn't have cell phones then, so there was no way to look up directions, hotels, restaurants, or anything else I would need. The only thing I booked before I left was a single front-row seat ticket to a Tori Amos concert in Albuquerque, New Mexico.

The trip was somewhat reactionary as I had recently broken up with my boyfriend and had been through a slew of incidents that caused significant turmoil and self-doubt. I had applied to three grad schools and didn't get accepted to any of them. I was in two car accidents nearly a month apart. I suffered a major concussion from the first, and in the second one I nearly totaled the rental car that I was using while my car was getting fixed from the first accident. Finally, I had recently been diagnosed with advanced cervical dysplasia. I was hitting a very low point.

I had started seeing an acupuncturist and was starting to feel immense relief from the car accidents. In working with the acupuncturist, I had started a comprehensive healing plan that included a cleaner diet, regular herbs and supplements, and becoming more aware of the connection between my mental and physical health through deep breathing and meditation. I began to feel a level of calmness and peace I had never experienced before, and I felt healthier than ever.

Unsure of the details, but equipped with a newfound sense of peace, I hit the road to figure out my life's trajectory. The trip was lonely, but it didn't bother me, as my head was full of content to digest. I stayed at a variety of hotels and saw my first concert alone, which was equally awkward and liberating. The last leg of my trip was to the Grand Canyon. The sights initially underwhelmed me, but as I ventured throughout the park, I found its vastness quite moving, and somehow I felt more connected to everything. As I was driving out of the canyon, the sun was setting, generating unworldly colors and ethereal images. An incredible sense of peace and accordance consumed me. I suddenly felt a deep connection to what felt like universal wisdom that I had never felt before. I felt a deep appreciation for people in my life and an extreme sense of forgiveness for those with whom I had felt either hurt me or let me down. In that brief and sudden moment, I understood the good intentions of all, and I was able to release myself from the burden of believing that I didn't deserve what I needed and wanted growing up throughout my life.

We all may have times throughout our lives where we take a risk or experience something out of the ordinary, and it can feel liberating and ultimately empowering. During fundamental changes throughout our lives, that empowerment in ourselves and in others who will experience the same change can be vital in tackling any responses to change that create resistance.

I have been on a long and continuous journey with empowering others throughout my life, personally and professionally. Growing up in a tremendously strict and authoritarian home, I have taken on some similar, controlling tendencies. I veered from the abusive and outwardly authoritative propensity as a mother, but can grapple with exhibiting dominant and controlling behavior at times that naturally clash with empowering others.

As a mom, I made it such a priority to abandon the abusive lifestyle my dad created throughout my childhood, that I ultimately became controlling and scripted in a desperate attempt to protect my daughter from anything similar to what I experienced. It turns out that I ended up creating obstacles for my daughter in my attempt to avoid them. Now that my daughter is grown, I can see I missed opportunities to let go, trust, and empower her to develop her own way of doing things and becoming her own true self. Now that she is an adult, I have finally learned to refrain from telling her what to do or how to do it. I have to let her figure that out on her own. Developing the skill to step back, listen, and support has been the most valuable thing I have done in empowering her to handle life and the various changes and challenges it presents.

This realization has transcended to my professional life, specifically with those we focus on to develop as leaders. Once the organization began to grow, we needed to focus on delegating administrative duties and nurturing leaders to ensure effective organizational operations. As I began to embark on this process, I subconsciously defaulted to a dominant and controlling approach in transitioning others to their new roles with new responsibilities. Initially, the interactions were based on a purely directive model where I tried to get them to do what I wanted them to, and sometimes they would and sometimes they wouldn't. This model required that I direct them regularly, to the point of micromanaging. The more I micromanaged, the more resistant they became to accomplishing tasks and initiatives on their own. The more they resisted, the more frustrated I became, and the ineffective cycle continued.

After a hectic season, we found numerous mistakes and oversights were made in the areas over which the newly appointed leaders were in charge. Because we were all so impacted, I was able to conduct my usual hounding. It turned out the oversight cost the organization over $1 million in revenue. It was at this time that I knew I had to do something different to enact change with the way the leadership team was responding to the changes in their new roles and responsibilities. Being controlling and micromanaging were not only ineffective in developing others within the organization, but it also cost the organization growth and revenue. After much reflection and research, I determined that the only way the organization and the individuals within it could grow was by developing relevant and attainable goals and empowering people to meet them using their own developed processes and work-style preferences. I developed a one-on-one system throughout the organization, along with quarterly evaluations, during which I utilized a coaching approach that included active listening and guiding each leader in solving problems on their own. This process of empowerment made an enormous impact, and the organization began to develop leaders that were confident in leading their respective key areas of the organization.

At times I may get overloaded or stressed and catch myself trying to control matters or micromanaging. I can always tell I am doing this by the way others react to it. They immediately seem stifled, and when I step back, we can find our way back to an empowered environment where we can adapt, and even pursue change while working towards the organization's goals.

Individualization

My older sister was very particular when we were young, and she was only comfortable with my mom or grandmother holding and caring for her. Like most of us, she was timid around my father and did what she could to avoid him. Once, when she was about three years old, she was at the park with my oldest brother, mom, and dad. When it was time to go, my dad picked her up to carry her out, and my sister spit in his face. He was so livid that he commanded everyone else into the car and left her at the park. As they were driving down the street, my mother got out of the moving car to retrieve her.

The amount of time we spent at the horse races as children had its disadvantages. Sometimes our parents dropped us off somewhere nearby for entertainment, such as the mall or the beach, but much of the time we were left to either entertain ourselves in the infield or sit in the seats and find ways to make watching horse racing enjoyable. The pitfalls of my father's gambling gravely impacted the emotional safety in our home. As a result, we all grew somewhat resentful of the time we spent at the track, except for my oldest brother. He always took an interest in the horses to share the time with our dad.

We loved Mexican food from anyplace, but when we found ourselves seated in a restaurant with a waitress and dimmed lighting, we knew it was a special occasion. With seven of us at a table, some of us kids would often end up seated at the opposite end of the adults. My brother in the middle often kept us laughing, and this time it was by filling the table candle with any item he could find to drop in until it burst into a large flame. We furiously put it out to avoid punishment.

We were all complete sugar fiends growing up. It was impossible to keep any candy or dessert safe from us pillagers. My father had to rely on his dictatorship to preserve his favorite treats. He kept much of his stash in the fridge and freezer, and it was made clear that if you touched it, you would pay. I came home one afternoon from our neighbor's house and found my youngest sibling, Jon, sitting at the bar with an array of sweet treats spread out in front of him, his face smeared by a mixture of chocolate and tears. The sight was horrifying, troublesome, and yet I felt a little envious. I asked him what he was doing, eating Dad's cookies and a variety of other chocolate treats. He muttered the explanation that he was caught sneaking one of dad's cookies from the fridge, and his punishment was to eat all the sweet treats left in the house.

I could feel my bare feet burning on the hot summer asphalt as my mom kept nudging me into a closer hug with my little brother. Going to the beach a few days each summer was one of the few things we did together as a family. We were required to get up very early, and then the seven of us would cram into the car. There was an enormous ice chest filled with food in the trunk to get us through the day, which would last until near sunset. These days were special, as my dad would stay out in the ocean and swim most of the day — he even invested the time to try to teach me how to body surf. On this particular day, my mom insisted on getting a picture of my younger brother and me hugging, which we weren't usually inclined to do. As much as we loved each other, we were often lumped together, and were somewhat separate from my older three siblings. With a six-year gap between me and my older siblings, I often felt left out of the closer connection my older siblings had with my mom. In particular, my sister and mom seemed to be confidants, and throughout my childhood, I never felt a part of that bond. I often did things alone or found friends to play with, and as I got older, I checked out completely.

I was on restriction during most of my teen years. I was constantly defying my father's strict rules, and as a result I was forbidden to go out anywhere with my friends. This didn't mean much to me as I would sneak out after they went to bed which created a constant game of cat and mouse between me and my dad. It certainly added to the stress for everyone else in our home. My parents went to bed quite early, so usually once they were asleep, I would venture out with friends. I was usually successful at sneaking right back in without any problems. Out of desperation, my dad would try a variety of approaches to keep me in, including installing an old-fashioned aluminum TV dinner tray booby trap (Google it, youngins) that would slam against the floor once I opened the door and would wake him up to extend my restriction time.

I have no idea how I ended up on homecoming court back in high school. As perplexing as it was, it was ultimately flattering for a young girl with little self-esteem. When we were assigned the task of attending the football game with a chaperone (your dad) and driving around in a car and waving, I couldn't think of anything that suited me or my dad less. My dad usually wouldn't attend anything that required him to be in the limelight in any way, but he agreed to go, and there are artifacts in the yearbook to prove it forever.

During the initial several counseling sessions I attended, my relationship with my dad emerged as a primary topic. After identifying a fractured and tumultuous dynamic, I decided to write him a letter to let him know it weighed on me. I wrote that I yearned for a close relationship and was sad that it was a challenge. I left the letter on his dresser, and several weeks later he sat me down and referred to the areas of the letter he highlighted to discuss. As we sat there talking, quite uncomfortably, I think we both knew a single letter wouldn't alleviate every obstacle.

These stories aim to offer a glimpse into how each of us approached our volatile upbringing. Based on our individual innate tendencies combined with the influence of our experiences, we each developed our own way of coping. My oldest brother maintained a tolerance and empathy for my dad, while my sister resisted much of his influence and gravitated toward my mom for care. My middle brother was often reserved and resorted to humorous antics, while my younger brother tended to grapple often with my dad's destructive focus. I often felt conflicted in that I desperately wanted a relationship with my mom and dad and usually pursued it, but I eventually became disgruntled due to a lack of attention from either parent. Though I attempted to reach out, I ultimately felt rejected and became defiant.

In revisiting the change adopters, it is interesting to plug my family in to the categories. Based on these stories of origins, I imagine it may look as below. We all vary and likely require a different approach or level of support.

Role	Family Member
Leader	Mom & Dad
Implementors	Oldest brother
Supporters	Middle and younger brother
Resistors	Sister
Defiants	Myself

Table 4.3 Change Adopters Within My Family

What worked for one sibling, certainly wouldn't have worked for another, and I am sure we each remember many things quite differently, based on who we are as individuals. Our personalities, tendencies, and origins continued to shape our ongoing experiences, creating our subjective realities, which are unique and differentiated from others.

Returning back to the categories of change adopters along with individualized responses to change efforts can assist in preparing for and navigating through a myriad of reactions and needs during such transitional times. As my organization has continued to grow, I have observed a wide variety of responses to change that I have been forced to acknowledge and support for change initiatives to be successful and sustainable.

How I approach an implementor or supporter may look very different to what support is provided to resistors or defiants. The one-on-ones I conduct with each lead team member incorporates a coaching approach. I engage in deep and active listening, and I provide the participant with opportunities to identify further issues they are experiencing. I reflect on their response to those problems and support their navigation to a solution. The change adopter categories at my organization would look like this:

Role	Response
Leader	Lead the change
Implementors	Administer directives and oversee change
Supporters	Compliant and buy-in to the change
Resistors	Resistant to the change
Defiants	Oppose the change

Table 4.4 Change Adopters at My Previous Organization

This approach requires a level of active listening that I do not always master, but when I can practice it, it works miracles in empowering others to adjust to change in their own, individual way. Not only does this generate solutions that will genuinely work for them, but it also helps to develop the leadership skill within them to adapt to change and ultimately create buy-in. They then begin to invest in the change and start to help others adapt themselves. It has proven to be a powerful practice to use within change initiatives and overall leadership development.

Creativity

I could feel my face pounding from the physical exertion and sweat seemed to be dripping everywhere. The Heatwave record had come to its end, and we debated which one to play next. The older siblings chose Stevie Wonder, and we carried on with our personalized hustle. I had no idea at the time, but at the ripe age of five years old, we were making a meaningful memory that would exemplify a vital outlet for my family and me throughout our young lives.

At times our home could be unpredictable, dark, and somewhat unnerving. We all navigated it quite carefully, but whenever music was playing, an enormous sense of relief and joy cleansed us all. From as early as I can remember if there was music playing in our home, everything was all right. Our family musical roots weren't dissimilar to those of 1970s cinema—honest, edgy, and as cool as possible. To anyone musically aware during the early '70s, we were of the Rolling Stones persuasion rather than the Beatles. We were drawn to almost anything rebellious and rooted in rock and roll. Since we lived in an all black neighborhood until I was in third grade, we appreciated (and still do) true soul music from a variety of authentic black soul artists.

My mom would often be locked in her bedroom blaring Marvin Gaye, Aretha Franklin, or Maxine Nightingale through the house. My dad would often be listening as well, frequently during a musical television show, turned up as loud as the old TV could go. As kids, we were often annoyed by it, but deep down, we were absorbing the joy and the freedom from our worry and uncertainty. We even went to concerts sometimes, and saw Chuck Berry, Sister Sledge, Bonnie Raitt, and others.

My oldest brother formed a band as a teenager, and it was like hitting the jackpot. Music filled our garage regularly, and watching his various bands perform throughout the years was a great form of entertainment. Loud rock would always be blasting from my brother's room, and rather than ensuring he turned it down, my mom would rush to his room, asking who the band was so she could listen to it again. We were all so proud of my brother and thankful for the joy his music brought to our home.

Being creative during any adjustment or change not only helps to ease the pressures of transition, it also allows for more in-depth consideration of individual tendencies and preferences. Creative outlets can make a changing environment more tolerable as it places creative control on the participants. If change participants have the creative space to accommodate the change in a way that makes it more palatable to them, it is far more likely that the change will be successful and sustainable overall.

After I graduated from high school, I faced a tough time in finding the interest or commitment to pursue anything. I bounced between potential careers, and shortly after I dropped out of fashion merchandising school, I pressed paused on everything and found a waitressing job to support myself while I figured out what to do next in my life. While I waitressed, I dabbled in a few general ed courses and came across a study abroad program in England. Though I was quite limited financially and not at all sure how such a costly and time-consuming endeavor would contribute to my overall life trajectory, I couldn't shake the need to go. I decided to move back with my parents for a few months, saved the money while waitressing, and finally went on an adventure to Europe.

I studied British History and Literature while living in England. During breaks, I was able to travel throughout Europe. Though on the tightest of budgets, I was able to visit seven countries and gain an experience that was unforgettable in every way. This creative break from the normal life I led in Southern California seemed to relieve many of the barriers I felt toward focusing on a path for myself as an adult. I visited places I had only heard of or read about. I observed a variety of cultures and ways of life. I learned how to live out of a backpack for weeks at a time. I figured out how to use public transportation to get from one country to another. I made connections by relying on others in a foreign setting. I figured out how to survive with a very short supply of funds, and I had many other valuable experiences. This creative break provided me with such inspiration that I felt motivated and exhilarated upon my return to pursue more in my life. Sometimes an unexpected, creative outlet helps initiate and commit to change in our lives.

At the time of writing this, we are nearly eight months into the COVID-19 pandemic quarantine, and when I venture out for essentials, I often see human behavior at an all-time peculiar and restless state. I've seen some very entertaining things and some that are quite questionable. In general, people seem agitated, but some people are exploring their creativity, both as a form of entertainment, and to maintain their overall mental health. Many are finding creative ways to manage the feelings they have about this major disruption to their previous lives. Learning a new language, taking on significant house projects (I have never seen Lowe's so full with people six feet apart from one another), baking, bike riding, walking outdoors, dying their hair outrageous colors, and conducting consistent in-home photo shoots are just some of the creative ways people are finding to cope. These types of diversions from the monotony keep us connected to something better than what we are doing and ultimately inspires us.

Creativity can make a world of difference in managing change in our lives. I have always found being in nature to be the ultimate way for me to renew my perspective, get grounded, and connect to my source of inspiration for stability. Music also channels an expressive origin for me and can always calm and ground me. I try to get creative while working with staff in an attempt to disrupt the monotony of meetings and recruit investment. I have found that food is a common pleasure and I tend to have a fixation of sorts on afternoon treats. For most meetings I try to bring in the latest goodies I have been hooked on to share. Sometimes I disrupt the usual meeting place and at the last minute arrange to meet at a restaurant to discuss items over lunch. People seem to respond well to this and it allows for some expression and commonalities outside of work tasks.

We all have vehicles that help moderate our reaction to things, especially change that can create such turmoil in our lives. Being creative in finding what works for us can be one of the most valuable things we can do during times of change. As a leader within my organization, I've often tried unexpected and unusual approaches to developing my leadership team.

Commitment During Change

The TRACK stage of Commitment encompasses the elements of empowerment, individualization and creativity and how they can impact our change efforts. Relying on these three elements during change can genuinely ground the change and prepare it for the next stage where true transformation takes place. This stage is reserved for the lighter, more expressive side of change that enables all participants to invest in the change in their own way and make it meaningful to them. Once that meaning is established through personal expression, the stage is set for sustainable change.

Commitment

- Empowerment: There are no shortcuts to acquiring the genuine feeling of empowerment. Whether feeling empowered is something we achieve on our own or an opportunity is presented to us form someone who believes in us, it can help individuals and teams grow tremendously. When a leader is genuinely dedicated to developing others, they are on the constant lookout for opportunities to empower others. I try to make it a weekly task to identify at least three staff members to present an opportunity for empowerment within my organization. Sometimes they take to it quickly and graciously. Other times, they may be hesitant or even generate excuses for accepting the opportunity. Those that pass up opportunities to be empowered are usually the ones I know I need to invest more time in.

- Individualization: Recognizing our individual origins and how they interact during a change process can help in establishing where our strengths can be used during the change and where we may fall short. That individual knowledge and how we apply it can be very powerful in enacting change. Each change participant has a role designed for them during a change process; it is just a matter of being aware of which role aligns to the right individual. Within my organization, I try to assign everyone possible a role in the change process in order to not only help with the heavy work involved in change, but to allow for individual expression and buy-in of the change. The more that the new norm represents the team who implemented it, the more fulfilling it will be for all.

- Creativity: Allowing for creativity in any change endeavor can lighten the strain of change and at times transform it to an enjoyable experience. Creating a culture that is safe to take risks and come up with ideas that may fail is key in generating a creative atmosphere. I have found that the more I can take my own risks and make public mistakes as a leader, the more I can model safety in taking risks with new and creative ideas which are critically needed during any change effort.

Reflection

> Explore a time in your life where you had to fully commit to a change in your life to see it through. Where did you find empowerment to get you through that process and how might you have relied on individual creativity to actualize the change?

Stage 5: Keep

The final stage of change is the most critical in ensuring that an implemented change is sustainable. This stage is where we revolutionize and evolve, ensuring we keep the change. Once change participants have gone through the stages of turmoil, regret, adjustment, and commitment, the stage is set for genuine transformation to take place. When a transformation is attained, the previous norm is relegated firmly into the past.

		TRACK/SHIFT Matrix	
	Stage	**TRACK: Participant**	
Deconstruct the Old Norm	1	Turmoil	Apprehension
			Fear of the Unknown
			Loss of Control
	2	Regret	Grief
			Disorientation
			Confusion
Construct the New Norm	3	Adjustment	Vision
			Communication
			Tenacity
	4	Commitment	Empowerment
			Individualization
			Creativity
	5	Keep	Revolutionize
			Evolve

JessicaSpallino

Table 4.5 Stage 5: Keep

Once transformation occurs regarding a change, participants become able to refer to the past and the old norm with a level of comfort and confidence. This level of ease enables the new standard to be fortified and often enhanced, making the old norm one that doesn't even seem plausible. It can be quite stunning to reflect on this phenomenon and how the human psyche can genuinely transform into new norms with a level of adjusted acceptance. With time and care during the five stages, transformation is empowered along with genuine, sustainable change.

Revolutionize

I didn't know how much my Honda CRX could hold, but I was determined to make a single trip when I left my childhood home. My dad never hit me until the age of 17, when I had become old enough to really challenge him. I can't remember what caused the scuffle, but before I knew it, he picked up my curling iron and hit my arm with it. It wasn't hard or harmful, but my feelings and pride were hurt, and at the age of seventeen, I handled it the only way I knew how. I packed my car and stopped at a friend's house to plan my next move.

Most of us eventually move out of the home where we grew up. Leaving home can be a very natural process, but in some cases, it can be tumultuous and indicative of the climate within the home we are leaving. For me, it was reactive, explosive, and poorly-planned. Looking back, I think I had just had enough of living under someone else's rules and needed to get out, however risky or unstable it was. I moved from place to place for several years, all equally disastrous, until I became old enough to understand that I'd have to buckle down and get a stable enough paying job to support myself while I tried to go to school.

My parents were never of the mindset to provide any means for their kids once they became adults, and we always supported ourselves and anything we wanted to pursue once we turned 18 years old. I ended up putting myself through college while waitressing and bartending, and up until I was in my late twenties, it was my only professional experience other than working in retail. After completing my first four years of college, I thought I wanted to be a teacher. I was always interested in teaching and had a deep interest in connecting with and helping students. Once I became a mother, I liked the idea of teaching even more, as it fits well with parenting.

When I started the teaching credential program, I was open and eager to learning what I could so that I would be as effective as possible once I started teaching. However, as the program progressed, I gradually realized that this particular facet of education wasn't going to be for me. Though I find the profession to be one of the most important in the world, and I'm sure it can be one of the most fulfilling careers, the standardized approach to teaching just didn't resonate with my personality. I understand that standardization is required in environments that are tasked with teaching thousands of students, I just knew it wasn't in alignment with how I was wired. I felt most comfortable and effective when the modality used for reaching others was more personalized. At that point, I had no idea what I would pursue within the space of education. I just knew it wouldn't be a classroom teacher. I still completed both my single and multiple subject teaching credentials, and I taught at my daughter's preschool while I explored options.

Late one morning during my daughter's dance class, I met another mom who was reviewing math curriculum. As we started talking, I discovered she worked as a curriculum coordinator for an independent study charter school. I had no idea what this type of education was or entailed, but I was intrigued. The next week I found myself sitting with her in her boss's office in an interview for a curriculum writing position. I didn't think it was possible to work from home and still exclusively care for my daughter, but within a week, I was writing pacing guides for elementary students, and the more I learned about the model, the more I loved it. This type of school served students who were not successful in the traditional school modality. The students enrolled in the charter school primarily worked from home with the ongoing support of teachers. I was impressed by this model, which was designed to serve those who struggled to learn in the traditional modality. I was completely inspired by the level of personalized support each student was receiving.

Many had severe obstacles that brought them to us, and I found helping those students to be ultimately meaningful.

Months later, my immediate boss left after a lot of turmoil with one of the founders, and I was asked to take her place. At this point, I hadn't even figured out how to complete my current duties, and I was now in charge of eight curriculum writers and the entire operation. Needless to say, I was in a bit over my head; I was forced to use the "fake it until you make it" approach. The executive director couldn't have been more supportive, but if she knew how overwhelmed I was, she might have reconsidered her decision.

As I gained experience through mostly making mistakes, I became more confident and started to grow in the role. My daughter was getting older, and I felt I could invest more time in the position and took the time to complete my master's degree in Administration. During this time, I became a complete maniac. I had newfound confidence: I implemented several new programs, managed three new teams, and brought new ideas to the lead team weekly. I never stopped thinking of new ways to serve our families and create success for the organization, though there seemed to be a culture that was intent on keeping things the way they had always been, and had a disappointing lack of consideration for the student's perspective. When we observed deficiencies in overall student performance, the reply was very often that the students were very fortunate; we were the last option for them, and because they were often disenfranchised, they would never perform better than they currently were. The low standard we had established for our students, and the even lower expectations we conditioned them to have of us, felt counter to the fundamental reason any of us are drawn to work in the field of education and it disturbed me greatly. There seemed to be a disheartening disconnect between the mentality of our lead team and the diverse students we served. I gradually became obsessed with overturning what I found to be an unethical culture that wasn't at all focused on the students, but revolved around the lead staff's limited ideology.

It turned out that there were maybe only a few that were terribly impressed with my work, but luckily, they were the ones that mattered. The executive director/co-founder, business manager, and I developed a tight three-person crew focused on growth and innovation for the organization. Unfortunately, the other co-founder and her team grew resentful and were threatened by the growth and continuous changes. The lead team quickly became divided into two distinct gangs, with one co-founder on either end. Due to my fierce preoccupation with fostering growth in the organization, I underestimated the power of the resistance to my overzealous change efforts.

I was taken aside on several occasions and warned to slow the pace of my efforts, but this only triggered my need to fight the resistance. So, I continued to do what I knew was right. My gritty and determined origin, handed down to me from my dad, was soon revealed, and a full-blown revolution was underway. After ongoing personal attacks and attempted maneuvers to either silence or push me out of the organization, we all sat down to discuss the issues my efforts at change had brought up within the organization. The opposing co-founder expressed her need for me to cease change efforts immediately or leave. What happened during that meeting was pivotal in the trajectory of the organization. The executive director/co-founder, my immediate boss, refuted her co-founder's claims that the changes being made weren't in the best interest of the students and the overall organization. This conflict created even further bitterness, and the opposing "crew" began to deteriorate due to the frustration and resistance to change within the organization. Many of them left due to the stress, never to return, and their complaints to the board and the school's authorizer prompted an investigation into the organization, which only revealed disgruntled employees about the leadership's renewed direction.

This harsh experience inspired my deep interest and passion in human resistance to change and just how fierce it can be. During this experience, I learned a lot about myself, my field, how change efforts work, and just how resistant others can be to it. It prompted my commitment to study and research response to change in a doctoral program. I have continued to apply my knowledge in my current personal and professional roles, and ultimately, to write this book. I believe my work with the response to change will be a lifetime effort, all prompted by this memorable experience. Shortly after the upheaval, I ended up leaving the organization that survived such a battle over change to diversify my professional experience. I don't know if the changes I implemented and the spirit of improving offerings and increasing expectations of the students has remained. Either way, pushing for change that one believes is right, even if it is faced with the most brutal opposition, can often be the most needed and rewarding change of all. There is a cost associated with every change, and this factor should always be considered when fighting for change. In this case, the sustainment of change can often be one of the most challenging aspects of change, which we will discuss in chapter seven.

During the COVID-19 pandemic, due to lingering social distancing recommendations and with schools and many businesses still closed, we see unprecedented changes to the norms in Southern California. Many businesses have transitioned its entire workforce to remote working conditions, and they are starting to look ahead on how to maintain this model in the long-term. Face to face service industries are figuring out new ways to conduct business moving forward. Restaurants are open, primarily with outdoor seating and the requirement to wear masks.

The California State University System transitioned to a complete online delivery and school districts have been primarily online for months, with some plans to reopen in the coming months, which may change. My organization transitioned to be fully online two years ago, and we have since developed our own online systems, including a comprehensive student information and learning management system and course catalog. Change has been forced upon us in the space of education. It will continue to be harder for some, likely based on their origins with change.

Though a challenging change, the transition to remote work has revealed some benefits. Traffic has decreased and the air quality has improved. Parents are now able to work from home and enjoy much more flexible schedules. Businesses can allocate resources to technological advancements, rather than funneling resources to buildings. This pivotal time can be a tremendous opportunity for a revolution in how we operate in the world. Depending on the organizational and industry culture, businesses can transform the way they conduct business, and we can reap the many benefits this shift may bring. Those with origins resistant to change and clutching tightly to the way they have always done things, will struggle. More fluid organizations that are built on ongoing change will likely thrive and lead their industries. It will be interesting to observe trends that formulate during this very transitional time.

Evolution

I bought the extravagant chaise lounge with my employee discount back during the days of my short-lived adventure working at my favorite store, Anthropologie. I never imagined I'd be cramming it into a friend's Toyota Land Cruiser, along with my favorite succulent plant that took years and years to grow. Yet here I was in the middle of a workday, gathering a few basics to fill my new apartment. When I brought my friend's car back to her, I think she hoped to get more info on the status of my personal life, but I was far too numb and likely in denial to discuss how my sixteen-year marriage was dissolving.

Later that evening, as I sat in an empty apartment with the chaise lounge, succulent, and a couple of bags of clothes, the reality of it all sank in. I felt utterly paralyzed with pain and sat on the bare floor, crying until early the next morning. I lived in several apartments throughout the following years while my daughter bounced back and forth between living at my place and the house she grew up in with her dad. Attorneys, paperwork, and a whole lot of raw emotion followed, along with trying to monitor my daughter during the peak of her volatile teen years. The pain and destruction often felt like far more than anyone could handle, though there only seemed to be the option to keep moving forward.

The details of my failing marriage are personal and not appropriate to share. However, the process with the most tumultuous change of my life is valuable regarding this discussion on change and, specifically, evolution. Based on my emotional development, or lack thereof, mainly due to my dysfunctional upbringing, I wasn't available for the emotional demands a marriage brings. However, I chose to get married and have a child at the age of 28. I became laser-focused on the motherhood part and neglected the wife part, as I simply wasn't equipped for the role. What ultimately transpired was a marriage committed to parenthood, but lacking in a healthy, evolving relationship.

When my parents both died, I struggled processing it, especially considering the tragic manner in which my dad passed. By this time, my marriage was functioning on an as-needed basis, and I had buried myself in my work and a Ph.D. program. I had no idea how to guide my pre-teen daughter through the painful and confusing process of losing my parents so tragically. When my dad died as he did, I initially attempted to keep the crushing details from my daughter until I could figure out how to deliver the information to her. Unfortunately, a family member told her all of the lurid details before I could gather myself to do so. I was still numb, in shock and pain, and I found myself completely shutting down. I felt as though the unrealistic frenzy I had created to protect my daughter from the reality of my capacity and upbringing, had suddenly expired. The harsh truth was out about my complicated origins, and there was nothing more I could do to protect my child from any of it.

What followed were several months during which I withdrew from being an active member in my home. I felt no one could understand what I was going through, and there was no point in trying. I finally allowed the chips to fall where they may, and they ended in divorce and a painful distance from my daughter, who was approaching 16 years old. Several painful years ensued, moving from place to place, battling deep feelings of failure, guilt, isolation, and even suicide.

After many years of counseling, healing, and time to renovate, I began to be able to function without feeling severe torment and apprehension. I began to feel like a renewed person. One I knew much better than before and one that finally had something to offer. I became available to build a new relationship with someone I cared about and to continue to work on the one with my daughter. It was as though the painful change I went through upon divorce was something I had to go through to continue to grow as the person I needed to be. Sometimes painful change works that way. If we wish to truly evolve and grow, challenging and painful change is sometimes necessary.

Drawing on my divorce as an example demonstrates how each stage of the change process plays a significant role during difficult change. Divorce has been one of the most painful experiences of my life, and I'm wary of trivializing it by categorizing the painful process that involved loved ones into rigid stages of change. I do, however, believe these stages are somewhat universal, and by observing that I hope to reveal our ability to survive painful change. Over time, our journey through these stages does get easier and seeing that might provide resolve for others in some small way. Any change, big or small, voluntary or involuntary, that we encounter can be applied to these stages. Creating the awareness of how we progress through the change can help the process become more meaningful, effective, and better prepared for the next time.

The COVID-19 pandemic has dramatically impacted all industries, and within the field of education it has been a forced change that no one was quite prepared for. Though public schools have been charged with the challenging and demanding task of going online, independent study online schools like my own have had to make very few modifications. We have experienced growth based on the fact that many parents are now working from home and able to oversee their child participate in an independent study program. The pandemic has prompted a potential shift in education that can be quite effective if the industry can genuinely evolve and allow it to become the norm. Many institutions are at different stages in the change process and are either still in fear of the unknown, loss of control, or even confusion, and may never reach the empowering stages of change. If the overall industry was able to navigate the stages of change proposed in this book and allow this new way to become the norm, they might be able to succeed in serving millions of students effectively during such a tumultuous time.

Keeping the Change

During the very dark time in my life after the loss of my parents, divorce, and career transition, I encountered and navigated every stage of change outlined below. Each and every step demonstrates the treacherous path to pure evolution, the final sensation of the change process, and the ultimate goal in the change process.

1. Turmoil

    - Apprehension: I was in a dysfunctional state within my family life, but I was unsure of what to do or how to do it. Sensing the needed change, but uncertain how to approach it or even imagine it.

    - Fear of the Unknown: Once embarking on the divorce process, I was terrified of what lay ahead and how I'd survive it.

    - Loss of Control: I felt a complete lack of control over nearly everything in my life, from primary relationships to daily life set up.

2. Regret

    - Grief: I experienced a profound sense of loss over a life built for over 16 years, loss of a primary relationship, and a familiar lifestyle.

    - Disorientation: I moved from place to place, feeling aimless and ungrounded.

    - Confusion: I was unable to make sense of life moving forward and struggled to understand the level of destruction created in my life.

3. Adjustment

    - Developing a Vision: I recognized the need to establish a constructive path moving forward and what my life could look like moving ahead.

    - Communication: I focused on communicating with those close to me and to the people involved so I could provide support and be transparent.

    - Tenacity: However difficult, I stuck with a healthy plan to move forward, and I avoided succumbing to discouraging thoughts or obstacles. I recognized that things would look different than they used to, and that is acceptable.

4. Commitment

- Empowerment: I focused on and celebrated wins and new developments to encourage further progress towards my new life.

- Individualization: I set goals and made progress at my own pace in a way that made sense and felt right for me.

- Creativity: I discovered creative ways to nurture and enjoy the new life path ahead of me. For me, this meant additional time outdoors, traveling, and writing.

5. Keep

- Revolutionize: I broke through and detached from old ways of doing things and developed new ways to live my life, specifically concerning personal relationship dynamics.

- Evolve: The new way of living my life with renewed relationship dynamics, lifestyle, and goals became the norm. I experienced a feeling of resolve with the new standard.

Reflection

> Evaluate a time in your life when you experienced true evolution through change. How did each TRACK stage contribute to you eventually evolving with the change and being grounded and at peace with the new norm?

Chapter 5: Origin Stories

Throughout this book, I've explored the connections made between formative experiences that involve rooted emotions and how they play out later in our lives as we experience dynamic change. Because of these deep emotional memories, or origins, individual responses within the proposed stages of change may differ significantly. We have also explored whether we are a change participant or a leader during change; leadership is the most fundamental determinant of successful change.

Considering the importance of our ability to lead, combined with our formative emotional origins during change, we might ask, "How do our origins interface or even conflict with our abilities to lead during change?" Many studies, including my own, have been conducted on leadership and its role during change. Rather than going too deeply into research at this point, I will simply include that studies have uncovered that the impulse and capacity to lead emanates primarily from innate abilities and early childhood experiences. It has also been suggested that effective leadership is linked to three conclusions:

1. Some aspects of leadership are natural, and some leaders may need to work harder to achieve effective leadership.

2. Effective leaders likely need to demonstrate hardiness, grit, and tenacity.

3. Authentic leaders build their practice outward from ingrained values and tendencies.

There are recent considerations on leadership that believe that the most effective leaders demonstrate a humble, hard-working demeanor that has little to do with charisma and everything to do with grit, tenacity, and commitment to a vision. This is a leadership style and approach that resonates with me, and when looking at my humble origins, it is not difficult to make the connection as to why that is. My roots lie in a working-class, liberal home that was significantly impacted by mental illness and volatility. My origins are pervaded with schizophrenia, bipolar disorder, anxiety, depression, and an ongoing battle with fear of abandonment. These origins are also infused with a scrappy, hard-working, and fight-for-what's-right mentality, and these all contribute to the unfolding of what I consider a somewhat unique life path.

My Personal Origins Summarized

Many of my origins are corrupted with fear, defiance, and overall turmoil. I often felt neglected and anxious as a young child, and once I hit my teen years, I rebelled entirely with no regard for consequences. After attempts to get some help and guidance, I realized I was on my own, and the following years were saturated with extreme drug use, over-drinking, and overall agitation with occasional glimpses of that young, tenacious girl searching for tennis balls. I no longer blame my parents for what they couldn't provide, as I too am a survivor of raising a teen, and we do the very best we can with what we're equipped with. In retrospect, as parents, we recognize that we've made mistakes and failed our own kids at times, and all we can do is move forward and learn as parents and leaders.

After I graduated high school, the pain and torment persisted. I ended up in unhealthy relationship after unhealthy relationship. I finally found my way to counseling and some ultimate healing. After an extended trip to Europe, college finally stuck, though I felt at odds with the overall system. I stumbled into marriage and became a mother, and I have never felt such a purpose in my life as I have with motherhood. We struggled financially and emotionally within our marriage, and I went back to college to become a teacher. Once educationally prepared for the position I studied for, it was clear that the traditional route wasn't for me. I found myself drawn to an alternative area within the educational field. I began working in the independent study corner of the educational world, utilizing online and blended learning modalities in the late '90s and have devoted my entire career to this unique space.

Origins at Play Within My First Organization

The first organization I worked for brought about one of the most trying, yet valuable experiences of my career. For the first time in my life, I faced my origins and how they interface with leadership during change. As the resident change agent, I not only encountered resistance but fielded aggression, manipulation, and hostility. Each stage of change from fear of the unknown and disorientation to developing a vision was met with fierce and destructive resistance and constant contention. As I reflect on this time, I am now able to recognize how the origins of each leader in place during this tumultuous time.

I felt under attack personally because of my change efforts, which prompted a feeling of profound responsibility to fight for what was right. The young girl with the tenacity to teach herself to roller skate took over, and I became committed to seeing the change through regardless of the fierce opposition. My dad often found himself at odds with opposing teams during his long career as a union steward pushing for change. However, he would sometimes go off the rails and create unnecessary damage. I found myself with the same intensity when fighting for what was right, just as I watched him do throughout my childhood, and this origin of mine played out during this transformative experience.

When observing the others involved during this change crusade, their origins may not be too difficult to identify. My primary opponent during the fight for change was the co-founder and assistant director who thrived on order, knowing what to expect, and controlling all aspects of the organization. Though her intentions may have been aligned to what she felt was right for the organization, it was influenced by a disposition of discrimination and low standards for the students we served. Any proposed change to make our program better and more useful for the disenfranchised population we served was met with the attitude that improvements weren't necessary. The rationale used to defend this stance was that the students came to the school as a last resort and that they were frankly lucky we were there to serve them. This mindset brought out a powerful drive in me to ensure our program was focused on what was best for the students and not the adults.

Reflecting on the assistant director's response to change during this time, I imagine some of her origins ran as deep as mine. It appeared she might have had similar ingrained emotions in regard to fighting for what she thought was right, however wrong I thought she was. She had a deep emotional connection to the organization that she co-founded and how she felt we should serve students, even if it seemed discriminatory from my perspective. Just as my origins compelled me to fight for the underdog, hers likely motivated her to protect those on top. The clash between our two strong views caused major turmoil for all involved.

In observing the executive director's potential origins, she is someone who avoids confrontation and addressing conflict. As opposing views were intensifying around her, she neglected to utilize the power of her leadership to find solutions until it became far too toxic to be control. Her kind, supportive demeanor, along with her tendency to avoid conflict, is likely a result of her origins. In fact, this conflict was not unique; she found herself in a variety of similar struggles that challenged her leadership and the entire organization, which are most likely due to her origins.

The business manager at the time became my sole confidant and source of support during the time of tumultuous change. We worked closely together to ensure effective changes were taking place for students, and we became far more reliant on each other during a time of extreme attacks and turmoil. Based on her origins, she was an analytical and calm thinker and approached such strife with emotional restraint and clarity. She was always the voice of reason and acted as an effective leader during this time. Her origins established a sense of logic and reliability, and she understood the importance of patience and composure during times of intense emotion and turmoil. She made the overall situation less destructive than it might have been and preserved needed change where it was desperately needed.

As I look back and reflect on this time and each leader's role during this fiercely intense time of change, it becomes clear that we all held origins that contributed to the way the process played out. It was a harrowing and stressful time, and as I've developed such a passion for this topic, it's clear just how troubling change can become. In reviewing the established stages of change, I can see that we all never made it past the first and even second stage of change. We remained in the stage of turmoil, filled with apprehension, fear of the unknown, and loss of control and only entered the second stage of grief with feelings of loss, disorientation, and confusion. The stages of commitment, reinforcement, and transformation only took place for some of us after several left the organization on stress, and those stages became severely compromised due to the experienced trauma the previous stages produced. We were able to implement some of the changes, but the critical stage of transformation was never able to firmly take place because of the damage that remained. I ended up leaving the organization before ensuring the final stages formalized and the new norms were established. Looking back, I believe this experience with change will forever be a part of the organization's origins and will always serve as a valuable lesson on how to be more effective at implementing change.

Origins Within the Educational Industry

The educational industry contends with change on an ongoing basis in regards not only to persistent universal reforms to improve student performance but also with the enduring diversification that continues to take place within traditional education. The introduction of charter schools, and in my experience independent study charter schools, has disrupted the conventional education system. When I started working in the independent study charter school space over 20 years ago, we were serving a direct need of our neighboring school districts. They all had a relatively small population of students who became severely at risk of dropping out of school for a variety of reasons and needed an alternative modality to get them either to graduate or become more successful in school.

We had a great relationship with the school districts as we had developed a mutually beneficial relationship. We were able to help their students who had either gotten into trouble, became pregnant, or had some other challenge, and we were able to gain enrollment that helped us survive as a small, independent organization. This worked for many years and still is in practice today. Throughout the years, however, this model began to gain popularity with more and more students and parents. It became not just a model of need, but a modality of choice. This ultimately created a new competitive landscape in education that had never existed before, and complications began to arise. School districts began to experience a decline in the enrollments upon which they had long counted. This decline impacted their budgets and challenged the ease of their survival. As a result, the relationship between school districts and charter schools became strained. To add to the tension, some unethical charter school leaders emerged, even with serious criminal charges, and the entire charter school industry became an area of suspicion and interrogation.

The educational industry as a whole is still vacillating between the first two stages of change—turmoil and grief—in regard to charter schools entering the space nearly 25 years ago. Many schools that have deep-rooted origins in the traditional approach to providing education have resorted to litigation and legislation to minimize the impact and growth of charter schools. In some ways, this has led to some incredibly unclear laws that dictate how charter schools can operate. However, in other ways, it has impacted the once-supportive and quite harmonious relationship between those charter schools dedicated to student success and the school districts. The result is a more limited choice for students who prefer or need a different modality in which to learn.

In observing leadership within the ever-changing educational industry, it appears that they continue to grapple with the first two stages of change: turmoil, and specifically the loss of control, grief, feelings of loss, and disorientation. The origins of many leaders working in traditional education, including the highly invested unions, are the central cause of the resistance to the changes in their environment. Maybe their origins lead them to feel territorial, like those of the assistant director with whom I battled. Perhaps they hold deep beliefs about the effectiveness of independent study or learning online. There are many possibilities, all of which would be worthwhile in understanding and addressing to ease the sharp division. Confining themselves to these two stages tends to serve only the leaders and neglects the student, who should be at the center of every decision made. If leaders on both sides of this school aisle could maintain focus on the student, there would be the capacity for the transition to the next three stages of change and land somewhere that ultimately benefits the student by allowing choice and diversification of options.

As a leader representing the charter school perspective, I have found my origins at play throughout the rising tensions between the two institutions. Often the feelings that arise are similar to those I experienced at the first charter school in which I worked. During a process of change, my compulsion to fight for what I believe is right with extreme tenacity emerges. My forcefulness is evident when conditions and standards feel unfair, simply because we are newer to the space and deliver something different than what has traditionally been offered. During these times, I may blog to express myself or look for ways to legitimize our industry through student growth and program initiatives. I have learned to use that same tenacity to work toward bridging the divide between the two, often opposing parties. I've also learned how important it is as a leader to provide the right amount of support during the first two stages of change, and if that is neglected, it will be impossible to gain collective acceptance and buy-in.

Students stand to benefit the most if we transition to stage three: commitment. In this stage, we can develop a new vision of how schools can operate and serve students in this new climate of choice. We could then evolve to stage four of reinforcement and work to empower all educators by individualizing support we all offer and allowing and encouraging creativity to not only compete within the new industry but provide options that appeal to students on a more personalized level. This could all lead to progressing to the final stage of change; transformation, where we have truly revolutionized how we collectively serve students and evolved as an industry, rather than holding fast to the ways we've always educated students. School choice has gained traction for a reason. If we embrace it as an industry, and together make our way through these stages of change, the more we can all provide effective solutions for all types of students.

Origins Within Other Industries

It is possible to identify origins within any industry. Based on deeply rooted emotions that inform long held beliefs, resistance to change within any industry or institution can be detected. Pharmaceutical companies within the medical industry, systemic racism within many institutions and regions, or sexism in male or female dominated industries, are just a few examples of where we can find origins at play.

Enacting change in any industry with resistant origins to change requires change agents with bold origins of their own along with an element of defiance toward the old norm. We will look at many examples of leaders in chapter eight that have challenged industries based on their personally held origins, combined with persistent and well executed plans for change.

Familial Origins

Other areas of my life offer valuable lessons on the impact our origins have on our ability to lead during change. As leaders within our own families, it can be critical to model constructive navigation through change. Growing up in my family and experiencing change brought about many feelings generated from the first two stages of change, including apprehension, fear of the unknown, disorientation, and confusion. With the lack of some fundamental leadership skills in my parents at times, change was often painful and worrisome. If there was a violent eruption, I never knew what was going to happen next, and I never felt confident we'd return to normalcy. Transition to the third stage of change, commitment, where a vision of a more functional home life was established, regularly communicated and enforced with tenacity, never truly happened, and we all became conditioned to a way of life with regular turmoil and grief. The change I continuously hoped for never happened, and I believe this explains my compulsion to sometimes move more quickly through the change stages than is ultimately effective.

Exploring my dad's origins can provide insight into some of his behaviors and tendencies throughout my life. He grew up with a very strict Italian immigrant father who approached parenting harshly and devoted most of his time working his way up in the company where he worked. He was forced to attend a Catholic school, which he loathed, and grew up in an overall conservative home that focused primarily on appearances. His father died when he was in middle school, and he completely rebelled when he became a teen. Though he respected his father's self-made, hard-working mentality, as an adult he maintained vehement defiance against all that he was forced to accept as a child. He pushed against anything that he felt was contrived or done for the sake of appearances. He resisted organized religion, any conservative notions, and anything or anyone that didn't recognize the underdog in any situation. Combine this defiance with an acute gambling addiction and an undiagnosed mental illness, and very often he seemed like a walking time bomb.

Some of my dad's traits are quite noble and admirable, while others make for a troubling upbringing. His role as a leader or patriarch within our family was complex and, many times, physically and emotionally abusive. He navigated through change quite precariously, and though I know he loved us and tried the best he could, these barriers kept a sustainable relationship with him from ever taking place. Once we all became adults and he had to allow us to be ourselves, it appeared to become too challenging for him. My mom was also quite complex, and though she had a softer, more accessible side, there were existent barriers that contributed to a challenging childhood. She never knew her father, and her mother was a single parent of two, who carried various jobs, including bartending and playing the drums for a band in the 1940s. My mom was left in a position to take care of both herself and her brother and suffered abuse from her mother's boyfriend. By the time she reached her teen years, she suffered from low self-esteem and depression. She then met a rebellious teen and, customary for the time, married and had five children immediately.

My mom had a beautiful and humble nature about her, and though she was the spiritual and emotional core of our family, she seemed mostly unavailable in my experience. My mom and dad first had three kids, then after a separation, reunited to then have me and my younger brother six years later. This pause in their relationship divided the five of us into essentially two separate groups of kids. By the time my brother and I came along, dynamics were well established. My mom and older sister had a close relationship, from which I always felt excluded. My mom often forced my sister to care for me when she couldn't, and my sister wasn't capable of doing this because she was just a kid surviving a complicated home herself. My older brothers kept to themselves as they were figuring things out the best they could, and my younger brother (who was later diagnosed with schizophrenia), and I were usually grouped together because we were just over one year apart. As the youngest, my mom tended to my younger brother as he was also a constant target for my dad's abusive treatment, and this left me feeling primarily on my own.

When my mom died suddenly, we were all shocked and devastated and found ourselves in a new place with my dad. He was at first very open to the support and reconnection to us all, and though stricken with grief and guilt, he remained in an open position for about a year. He wavered between the first two stages of painful change, feeling loss and disorientation. He slowly disappeared and was unable to be reached, and then about a year later, when he took his own life. I can't attempt to explain my dad's or anyone else's decision to commit suicide, but I can try to understand better the desperate position he may have been in considering his deep origins and the stages of change in which he was stuck. From my perspective, he seemed unable to launch himself to the third stage of change, which begins to turn the change toward a positive, constructive, and renewed position after my mom's passing. Maybe he wasn't able to get there due to his origins, his illness, and the lack of capacity to recover from such grief. I will forever reflect on this and hold the tragedy deep in my heart as an origin of my own.

As I reflect on myself as a family leader and how I've navigated through my parents' deaths, my divorce, and other challenges throughout my life, I have discovered many links to my origins. Some have contributed to a healthier progression through the stages of change, and others have created obstacles. I struggled immensely with the death of my parents and looking back I had a tough time getting through all the stages of change with them. My dad's death was especially difficult and brought up many issues, not only with the pain, grief, and confusion around it but also with my tendencies that could often mimic his. I, like he used to, completely shut down, and had no idea how to communicate, reach out, or lean on others during such dark pain. I buried myself in work, alienated myself from others, and became far less available to my daughter. It all resulted in the breakup of my marriage, which already had chronic issues, and tumultuous teen years for my daughter. In many ways, my origins caused me to fail in areas of my family, but luckily other origins in tenacity have helped me see things through to the final stages of the change of losing my parents and divorce.

During a time of quarantine and social distancing during the COVID-19 pandemic, a video was released of a black man being killed by a police officer in Minneapolis who was kneeling on his neck while he was detained for supposedly using a counterfeit $20 bill, as he pleaded for his life saying that he couldn't breathe. On the heels of restlessness from living in quarantine, the entire country erupted in protests and rioting, releasing pain, frustration, fear, confusion, and disorientation. As many express their support, sorrow, and position on exhibited racism in this country, change is what they are ultimately seeking. At this time, the four officers have been charged with murder. However, those opposed to racism are pushing for systematic change that goes beyond this single incident.

Fundamental changes regarding racism in our country will require us all to find our way to the next stage of change. We must move beyond turmoil and grief and into the stage of commitment, where we collectively develop a vision of equality within our country, communicate it, and work with tenacity to achieve what we seek. It will work into the fourth and fifth stages of change of reinforcement and transformation, where we empower one another, get creative, and truly evolve as a country toward this persistent issue. At this time, the persistent and widespread protests taking place over police brutality against black people are generating change momentum. If this momentum continues, states like Minnesota, that have started to revise policies on police treatment, will evaluate and change their practices. Congress will consider the police reform bill recently drafted aimed at ending excessive use of force to identify, track, and prosecute police misconduct.

This sort of transformation can't take place without addressing the origins of leaders across all positions on this issue. One of the biggest challenges to solving this problem is the deeply-held origins on this issue some may bring. Without addressing and dismantling these origins and configuring a new vision of equality, we will continue to struggle with institutional racism. As we continue to examine how leaders navigate through change, considering the infinite origins we all bring, we must ask which origins we each rely on to support our navigation through change and which create barriers. Most importantly, how do we best utilize our origins as leaders in helping others navigate through change and work at dissolving those that create barriers?

Further Origins at Play

We all have origins that play out to some degree during change, and more specifically, while we are trying to lead through change. Our origins can resist change and keep us in a holding pattern during the first two stages of change that take place. If we aren't able to eventually advance past the first two stages, then real change isn't possible. Some of us may struggle with change but hold origins that help us to persist through the very challenging times and fight our way to the stages that make change sustainable. Others may possess origins that respond very well to changing and dynamic environments and become agents of change and change leaders. The following examples from sports, music, social justice, and science illustrate how a person's origins affect the decisions they make and the routes their lives take.

Sports

Jerry Sloan devoted 45 years of his life to the NBA as a player, scout, assistant coach, and head coach. He was the longest-tenured coach in professional sports, and upon retiring after 26 seasons he held the fourth winningest coach in NBA history and endured much change throughout his term as coach. Throughout his career, he relied heavily on his deepest origins, which made him so impactful and memorable upon his passing in May 2020 at the age of 78.

Sloan's origins were on an Illinois farm. He was the youngest of ten with a humble, tough, and hardworking background. His father died when he was four years old, which created an even harsher situation for his family, who grew and hunted much of their food. As a child, he woke up at 4:30 each morning to complete farm chores and then walk nearly two miles to get to school in time for 7:00 a.m. basketball practice.

Sloan was a two-time All-Star player during his 11-year career with both Chicago and Baltimore, and is referred to as the "Original Bull" —he was the first Chicago Bulls player to have his jersey retired. He started his coaching career as an assistant coach with the Bulls and then onto head coach for nearly three years. After the Bulls let him go as a coach during the third season, Sloan took a break from basketball for almost three years and returned to his Illinois farm. He was later hired as an assistant coach for the Utah Jazz. Four years later, he became the head coach and general manager to eventually become a Hall of Fame coach as the fourth winningest coach in NBA history and leading the Jazz to playoffs every season, but three out of the over 22 he coached them.

In many ways, Sloan never departed from his hard-working, modest, farm origins. Even after he became an established and well-paid coach, he'd often drive an old van and would return to his Illinois farm each offseason to work the fields every morning. He's been referred to as the don't-mess-with-me, Clint Eastwood of basketball, and applied his tough, authentic, and hard-working origins to his leadership as a coach. He demonstrated genuine respect for the game along with a pragmatic view of it and fought against the self-focused, star-oriented culture that often permeated the game. He insisted on nothing less than intense effort and ultimate discipline. In utilizing his down to earth origins, he refused to bench and rest his star players, claiming that people who worked jobs much harder than playing basketball, paid money to see them play.

He demanded a work ethic and standard from his players that was at the same time conventional and refreshing, which earned him deep respect but with a bit of cautiousness. He required players to wear the same color shoes, jerseys tucked in, and assigned bench seating. Basketball star Karl Malone once challenged him, claiming he was going to wear a different color shoe from the rest of the team, and Sloan simply denied it. Sloan's origins refuted glory and demanded teamwork, and through his commitment to classic basketball, his origins made him an effective and novel leader.

Music

When Dave Grohl was seven years old, his parents divorced, and he grew up with his mother in North Springfield, Virginia. At the age of twelve, he began to play guitar. After growing tired of taking lessons, Grohl taught himself to play and eventually started playing in bands with his friends. With an initial profound influence of new wave music from his older sister, he heard punk rock for the first time when he was 13 years old and became an enthusiast. After playing in a variety of local bands and transferring to several different high schools, Grohl discovered his love for drumming. He taught himself by listening to Rush and Punk Rock records.

By the age of 15, Grohl's passion for music was formed and he couldn't imagine himself pursuing anything else. At the age of 17, Grohl lied about his age to be considered for the drummer of a local Washington, D.C. band, and when they asked him to join, he dropped out of high school and began to tour. He eventually met Kurt Cobain and Krist Novoselic at a Melvins concert through a mutual friend and band member. When Grohl's current band dissolved, the same friend referred him to Cobain and Novoselic as their band, Nirvana, was looking for a drummer.

Grohl joined Nirvana as their drummer, the band eventually signed with DGC Records, and in 1991 they recorded their iconic album *Nevermind* at Sound City Studios in Los Angeles. Upon the album's release, it was an enormous worldwide success, exceeding all expectations, and Nirvana became one of the most recognized bands in history and inducted into the Rock and Roll Hall of Fame in 2014. During Grohl's time in Nirvana, he continuously wrote and recorded his music and increasingly contributed to Nirvana's songwriting. Nirvana's frontman, Kurt Cobain, struggled with heroin addiction, chronic depression, and fame throughout his time with the band, and just a couple years after their breakthrough album, he was found dead in his home from a self-inflicted shotgun wound to the head in 1994. Cobain has been repeatedly ranked as one of the top 20th guitarists and voices of all time.

Grohl's next move was uncertain. He took some downtime and then entered the studio in 1994 and recorded a 15-track demo in which he played all of the instruments himself. He had the makings of a breakout album. Though he felt committed enough to it to turn down offers to fill the role of drummer for other projects and bands such as Tom Petty and the Heartbreakers, he began to experience resistance and criticism to be a frontman. He was known as the drummer of one of the most famous bands of all time, backing Cobain. Nirvana and alternative rock music fans initially had a difficult time not viewing Grohl as a replacement for Cobain, especially after such a tragedy and criticism ensued.

At this point, Grohl defaulted to his origins at a time during major change. He had transitioned from stages one and two of change of feeling loss, disorientation, and confusion. Grohl had started developing a vision for what he could be and contribute to the world of music, yet experienced resistance from fans. He relied on a genuine passion for life and love for music, and through refining his vision he further developed his vision and relentlessly communicated it with it until fans began to appreciate Grohl as a musician in his own unique right. Once he and his new band, Foo Fighters, were signed with Capitol Records, he continued through stage four of change, by utilizing his creative and authentic origins to become a legitimate and genial frontman and musician.

With his innate tenacity and passion for music, Grohl evolved as a true leader as part of stage five during the challenges his new band faced. Grohl had to make a tough decision while recording their second album, where instead of playing guitar, he also played the drums, and ultimately he decided to replace the band's current drummer. He faced further challenges when other band members announced their retirement or suffered issues with drug abuse. During these times, he evolved as a genuine leader, relying on his passionate and caring origins to support them all in becoming a unified and committed band. Grohl and many other bands within their genre have encountered a transition within the music industry from a rock and alternative sound that exemplifies authentic recordings with live instruments to a more manufactured and digitally recorded sound. Grohl's tenacious and authentic origins have placed him as an amiable leader in the preservation of rock music in its pure form. He purchased the '70s-era Neve 8020 analog recording console known for its proliferation of the raw sound of vintage rock and roll to conserve its rightful roots in music. He is also a known advocate for youth musicianship and contributes to the movement on an ongoing basis. Grohl has truly transformed into an active and inspiring leader as he continues to apply his deepest origins to this unique space. Grohl's origins have served him in challenging the music industry by maintaining some of its deepest roots.

Social Justice

Bryan Stevenson grew up in Milton, Delaware, in the 1960s and spent his early years at a "colored" elementary school. Though desegregation was enacted shortly after his first grade year, the old rules of segregation were hard to shake. Black and white kids played separately. Backdoors were used by black people when entering certain establishments, and community facilities were still informally segregated. When Stevenson was 16 years old, his grandfather was killed during a home robbery. Though he thought the murderer's life sentence seemed just, he felt that because his grandfather was older, it seemed exceptionally cruel, even though his fundamental belief is that redemption should be valued over revenge. Stevenson found solace and direction from the African Methodist Episcopal Church, which he attended as a child, where he played piano, and where he sang in the choir. It was within his church that he developed a strong faith and belief that each person in society is more than the worst thing he's ever done.

Stevenson was active in high school. He played sports, served as student body president, and refined his arguing skills in his home growing up with his brother and went on to win American Legion speaking contests. Earning straight A's won him a scholarship to Eastern University, and he went on to earn a master's degree in Public Policy and a law degree from Harvard Law School. During law school, he worked for Stephen Bright's Southern Center for Human Rights, an organization that represents death-row inmates throughout the South, and during his work there, he found his calling. He graduated and moved to Atlanta, Georgia, where he joined the Southern Center for Human Rights and was assigned to run the Alabama resource center and death-penalty defense organization, funded by Congress. When Congress funding was eliminated for death-penalty defense, Stevenson founded the non-profit Equal Justice Initiative in Montgomery. With Alabama representing the highest per capita rate of death penalty sentencing and being the only state that did not provide legal assistance to people on death row, his venture was able to earn grant funding. Based on Stevenson's origins of valuing redemption over revenge, he focused on representing those who committed crimes as children and who were subject to excessively harsh sentencing. In 2005, the U.S. Supreme Court found that the death penalty was unconstitutional for persons convicted of crimes under the age of 18 in the case Roper v. Simmons. Stevenson relied on his innate sense for fighting for those he felt were in need and set about a litigation campaign to gain a review of all cases where children were sentenced to life without parole. In a landmark decision, Miller v. Alabama, the U.S. Supreme Court ruled that mandatory sentences of life without parole for children 17 and under were unconstitutional, impacting 29 states and 2,300 children nationwide.

Stevenson has devoted his life and career to this cause, and though unpopular and controversial among some groups of people, his strong origins generated change in individual lives, overall communities, and even within the criminal justice system. By 2016, Stevenson had saved 125 men from the death penalty and represented defendants living in poverty and those on appeal for wrongful convictions. His deep origins in redemption and an institution that fairly represents all has helped to alleviate prejudice within the criminal justice system.

Science

Though born in Paterson, New Jersey, Kathryn Sullivan considers Woodland Hills, California, her hometown. She graduated from high school in 1969 and earned a Bachelor of Science Degree in Earth Sciences from the University of Santa Cruz in 1973 and went on to earn a Ph.D. in Geology from Dalhousie University in Nova Scotia, Canada in 1978. During work on her Ph.D., she participated in several oceanographic expeditions that studied the floors of the Atlantic and Pacific Oceans. By the time she completed her degree, she had secured a fellowship offer to continue her exploration of the Atlantic in deep submersebles.

Sullivan's career path for oceanography and Earth studies is grounded in her innate curiosity and passion for exploring the unknown. As a freshman in college, she was required to take three courses outside of her major, one of which was a marine biology course. During that course, she was required to read the memoir *Great Waters* by Sir Alister Hardy, and she found that the oceanographers in the book led the type of life she dreamt of as a child, one that was full of inquiry, the outdoors, exploration and adventure. From there, Sullivan became hooked and transferred her major from Linguistics to Earth Sciences. The science courses she took throughout her college years revealed a more hands-on experience out in the field versus an inside a laboratory that she had expected, and it enabled her to travel to exciting places to explore and learn about the planet.

This path was an excellent fit for Sullivan, based on her origins and beliefs that we all have natural tendencies to want to make sense of the world in which we live and feed our innate curiosities. Sullivan has a passion not only to master a skill or become an expert on a topic, but her origins are also motivated by learning about other fields, including the arts, policy, and culture, and that making the interconnections is essential. She believes that seeking experiences and opportunities where we are out of our comfort zones and even scared to a degree is ideal for our minds to be fully alive and functioning. Sullivan thrives on the adventure of these experiences. She finds value in surrounding herself with genuinely good people, seeking mentors that may be different from ourselves and is cautious of the highly critical inner voice that can often limit our beliefs or abilities about ourselves.

In 1978, NASA had evolved from a seemingly militaristic organization aimed to win the space race into the more scientific civilian-friendly, an institution it is today. Previously, most astronaut members had come exclusively from the ranks of military test pilots, and the office opened recruiting efforts to include civilian researchers needed to contribute to the development of the upcoming space shuttle. Immediately after graduate school, Sullivan's origins led her to her first serious job and interviewed to become an astronaut. At age 26, she had claimed her first full-time job as an astronaut as part of NASA's eighth class of astronauts, nicknamed the "Thirty-Five New Guys." It was the first new group that represented NASA's first step toward a more diverse astronaut group, which included six women, three African American men, one Asian American man, and the rest white men. As an astronaut, Sullivan made her way out of the shuttle to become the first American woman to float freely through space. Sullivan trained, studied, and supported future missions for the following six years, spending more than 530 hours in space over three missions and considers her contributions to the work of the Hubble Space Telescope, her most enduring work.

In 1988, Sullivan joined the U.S. Naval Reserve as an oceanography officer stationed in Guam and retired with the rank of Captain in 2006. In 1993 she accepted a nomination from President Bill Clinton to serve as the chief scientist at NOAA to focus on Earth's oceans and atmosphere where she oversaw projects that involved ocean biodiversity and climate change. Sullivan then served as president and CEO of a science museum in Columbus, Ohio, and then returned to NOAA under Barack Obama and unanimously confirmed by the Senate as the agency's deputy administrator. She later served on the Pew Oceans Commission, whose work influences the U.S. ocean laws and policies governing the preservation of ocean wildlife and prevents the collapse of ocean ecosystems. In 1985, Sullivan was appointed by President Reagan to the National Commission on Space, where she contributed to the report, entitled "Pioneering the Space Frontier," which outlined goals for U.S. civilian space activities for the next 25 years. Sullivan acted as a fellow of the American Association for the Advancement of Science and the American Institute of Astronautics and Aeronautics. She is a member of the Woods Hole

Oceanographic Institution, the Explorers Club, the Society of Woman Geographers and Association of Space Explorers.

In the Spring of 2020, Sullivan's origins of deep curiosity and commitment to living out of her comfort zone led her on an expedition to the bottom of the Challenger Deep, the deepest known point of the ocean. This expedition further procured her a pioneer as the first woman to reach the deepest known point of the ocean and the first person to travel to both Challenger Deep and space.

Sullivan's leadership and contribution to the overall advancement and conservation in space, earth, and ocean science are far-reaching and set the stage for her continued work and many to follow. Her origins reveal a profound curiosity about the world around her. Her refusal to concede to self-doubt is an inspiring example, and her indifference to disadvantages she has faced as a woman in her industry offers us a prototype for how to lead through change.

These four leaders demonstrate a personal style and approach to leading change based on their origins and have provided true inspiration for me as a leader. Through these four and other examples provided in this chapter, we can see how every individual utilizes their origins to lead others, especially while enacting change. We can observe through these examples that there isn't necessarily a single technique in leading others. Instead, an approach that incorporates our lived experience allows us to utilize the strength of our origins and also continue to work on the portions of our origins that create barriers to successful leadership through change.

Reflection

> Reflect on any leader you admire and think about how their origins have contributed to their accomplishments.

Chapter 6: SHIFT: Leader in Action

When combining personal origins, research, and practical examples of leading through change, it becomes apparent just how challenging it can be to lead others through change successfully. Based on this compilation of factors, change can be difficult to acquire and nearly impossible to maintain without an effective plan suited to the change that is being pursued.

	Stage	TRACK: Participant		SHIFT: Leader	
Deconstruct the Old Norm	1	Turmoil	Apprehension	Support	Prepare
			Fear of the Unknown		Inform
			Loss of Control		Appoint
	2	Regret	Grief	Help	Counsel
			Disorientation		Organize
			Confusion		Confirm
Construct the New Norm	3	Adjustment	Vision	Imitate	Guide
			Communication		Connect
			Tenacity		Persist
	4	Commitment	Empowerment	Fortify	Invest
			Individualization		Listen
			Creativity		Diversify
	5	Keep	Revolutionize	Transition	Challenge
			Evolve		Transcend

JessicaSpallino

Table 6.1 TRACK/SHIFT Matrix

The most challenging times I have had with change throughout my life have been when there is no plan or process in place to accommodate myself or others through the stages of change: Turmoil, Regret, Action, Commitment, and Keep. The more awareness, consideration, and plan for navigation through the stages of change, the more amicable, effective, and sustainable the change becomes. Developing a flexible model to lead others within their origins through change can be beneficial in creating a more effective process.

I have proposed a variety of activities, processes, and systems to navigate through each stage of the change process, particularly while leading through it. As previously discussed, SHIFT provides an action step for the leader to follow in response to the stages a participant experiences during TRACKAs a leader in any scenario plans for change, SHIFT can help to inform processes and tools to utilize during each stage to ensure the change doesn't get derailed by the diversions ORs can bring during formative stages of change.

Considering Change Adopters

When preparing for change as a leader it is imperative to effectively plan for all stages within the deconstructing phase and the constructing phase. It can be incredibly useful as one begins planning to inventory the participants and identify where they fit as a change adopter within the categories. From my experience, most leaders can readily categorize each and every staff member in regard to their change friendliness because the symptoms of each are easily detectable. For those whose categories aren't as readily apparent, informal surveys or one-on-ones can help in gathering enough data to identify each participant's capacity for change.

Ideally, the work of knowing each participant well enough to categorize their change dispositions is established throughout normal everyday practice as a leader. This happens through observations during regular meetings, one-on-ones, coaching, and monitoring during implementations. Building relationships with change participants before any change implementation, however minor or substantial, is what every leader should strive for to develop a strong, collaborative culture that can accommodate and pursue change. Additionally, developing organization wide goals or objectives with key results can help to justify change implementations and create expectations and accountability across the organization.

Key actions derived from SHIFT are outlined below per change adopter category, and though not at all exhaustive, they can provide some ideas on how to manage each change adopter. For example, keeping the change implementors empowered with information and appointing oversight tasks is imperative during change. Equally, investing the time to listen and diversify where needed for the change supporters helps to strengthen change efforts to reserve time needed to address the resistors and defiants. Identifying the resistors and defiants early on helps to prepare for the time and resources needed to keep them engaged in the change. Resistors need ample guidance and ultimate tenacity not only from the leader, but from the implementors and supporters as well. Though likely based on their own ORs, resistors may never be thrilled by the change, but may be able to join the change and eventually contribute to its success.

The defiants, however, can cause serious damage not only to the change effort, but to the overall organization and any established change-friendly culture. It is important that the leaders, change implementors, and supporters are all keenly aware of the defiants and their ongoing actions and commentary regarding the change. In extreme cases, defiants can be so destructive that they can infect not only the resistors, but the supporters, implementors, and can even divide leadership if vulnerable to negative influence.

Role	Adopter Trait	Needed Action to Support
Leader	Leading the change	Plan
Implementors	Administer directive and oversee change	Prepare, Inform, Appoint, Invest, Listen, Diversify
Supporters	Compliant and buy-in to the change	Counsel, Organize, Confirm, Invest, Listen, Diversify
Resistors	Resistant to the change	Guide, Connect, Persist
Defiants	Oppose the change	Listen, Diversify, Challenge, Transcend

Table 6.2 Supportive Actions for Change Adopters

Experiencing extreme change-defiant behavior as a change agent is one of the most stressful encounters of my professional career. If defiance has been continuously addressed and treated with the actions of SHIFT and the destructive behavior continues, it can become evident that the ORs of the defiants are too severe for the organization as a whole and tough decisions may need to be made. When change defiants persistently destroy efforts of all those within in an organization working toward the change, and interventions have been consistently employed, the only solution that remains is to let the defiants go. Leaders are often tasked with the tough decision whether to continue to allow destructive behavior or remove it for the sake of the overall organization and those working diligently towards the overall outcomes.

In my experience, if existing leadership is fragile and change defiants are strong, the clash can impact the overall success and culture of the organization. Change ultimately needs to start with strong leadership prepared for any level of change adopter, which needs to be willing to make tough decisions regarding the extreme defiants. Planning for every change participant, including consideration of their known ORs and change adopter categories, is critical in preparing for change and will ultimately propel the change's success.

SHIFT: Leader in Action

Phase 1: Destructing the Norm

These first two stages of Turmoil and Regret represent the process of deconstructing the norm before the change. Counsel and support are critical during this phase to ease the emotions that arise while letting go of old norms. Ample time is needed during the change process to deconstruct patterns and support the origins of those that struggle during this phase. Proper care and awareness are required to successfully transition to the second phase of constructing a new norm.

Stage 1: Turmoil — Support

The first stage of change can generally be the most tumultuous as it triggers the deepest and most resistant origins. When change is initially presented, the response is more often resistant than eagerly accepted. What usually follows are feelings of apprehension, fear of the unknown, and loss of control, and it becomes critical to address and counsel through these emotions so that they don't take hold, gain momentum, and take over the change efforts. If this stage isn't approached with awareness and care, the transition to the next phase becomes impossible.

	TRACK/SHIFT Matrix		
	Stage	SHIFT: Leader	
Deconstruct the Old Norm	1	Support	Prepare
			Inform
			Appoint
	2	Help	Counsel
			Organize
			Confirm
Construct the New Norm	3	Imitate	Guide
			Connect
			Persist
	4	Fortify	Invest
			Listen
			Diversify
	5	Transition	Challenge
			Transcend

JessicaSpallino

Table 6.3 SHIFT Stage 1: Support

Apprehension — Prepare

Whether planned or unplanned, change can initially create varying levels of apprehension and worry. One of the best ways to prepare for this is to be aware of it and the many forms it may take, based on an individual's origins. Worry can cause a wide range of responses physically and behaviorally, from minor to quite severe. There may be some people who are impacted by the proposed change that is rooted in anxiety when it comes to change, and others that may possess origins that thrive in it. It is the leader's responsibility to get to know how these people might react as much as possible, because then support through the change can be personalized, even within large organizations. During this stage, and if leading others, it's essential to watch for these signs in others and counsel others accordingly.

This is a great time to observe others as often as possible for signs of stress, and plan one-on-ones meetings or other forms of private meetings regularly so that change participants have a safe place to express their worries, concerns, and overall stress. These individual meetings can uncover triggers for behavior that they may not have even been aware of and can create a collaborative relationship between leader and change participant. Building these collaborative relationships becomes the foundation from which you will work as progress through the change stages develops. This form of supportive communication must be established at the very beginning of the change to ensure it is there to fall back on throughout all stages of the change.

Fear of the Unknown — Inform

Lack of information about change can often lead to misinformation and quickly turn to sabotage if the information isn't provided whenever possible. Humans have a deep inherent need to know what to expect and how things will impact them, and without it, the response to change can be quite destructive. Adverse reactions can often be avoided quite easily with the power of information. Even if the significant elements of the change and how it will impact others may be unknown, it can become a forum for trust and communication where information is shared as soon as available, and the unknowns can be explored continuously. Otherwise, the risk is taken for those in need of control to make their own assumptions about the change to avoid grappling with the discomfort of not knowing.

Developing a communication forum to track and share ongoing developments with the change can often appease those with strong origins that counter the unknown. Ensuring that ample research and preparation are in place for the change can help with anxiety about the unknowns of the change. As with any stage or emotion in response to change, it is important to watch for people who may be struggling to provide more in-depth information for those that need it and establish a safe place where they can express their conflict with this stage. Counseling those who feel at odds at this stage can make or break the change process. It is wise to address participants who may turn against the change effort because they lack information and preparedness.

Loss of Control — Appoint

Those with origins that create disaccord with losing control can be the most disruptive during change efforts. Those in need to be in constant control can exhibit forceful behavior and create fierce opposition toward those working to implement change. This resistance can often manifest in the form of hostility and ultimately infect all others involved in the change. I hold origins in this area and have spent a lifetime working on improving my symptoms with losing control. Releasing the need for control with those that carry origins here is not easy and is a process. Detecting those with deep origins is a great first step when leading others through change, and once identified, assigning them areas to hold some control throughout the change can turn them into your biggest advocates for the change.

I often think of myself as Labrador Retriever when it comes to change. Labs are always at their best and easiest to manage when they have an assigned job or task. Without a job, they are likely to chew up the bumper of your car or your living room wall, but once they have a ball to chase or frisbee to catch, they are the best performers you'll ever see. Just like hunting for tennis balls, if I have been assigned a job during any transition and have some control over some aspect of the process, then my anxieties are immediately calmed, and I am free to perform at my highest capacity. While conducting an inventory of teams you may be leading during change, identifying those that struggle most with losing control is critical. This can be accomplished through in-person interactions, one-on-ones, team meetings, or even ongoing surveys you distribute to continue to capture the climate of others during the change. Once you have acquainted yourself with those grappling with losing control, assigning them appropriate duties within the change can modify their resistance almost immediately. Recruitment is the antidote for those becoming disgruntled with losing control. Once direct involvement has been achieved, you may find they become the biggest supporters for the change, and much of your promotional work for the change will be done for you.

Case in Point

During the COVID-19 pandemic, and at the time of writing this book, seat-based schools throughout the country have been fully transitioned to virtual schooling. Many schools and teachers have struggled with this transition due to a lack of time to learn a new teaching modality, a lack of resources, or an overall resistance to the change. As a result, students aren't engaged or motivated, and are either not showing up for virtual classes or not completing their work. This is putting a further strain on these schools, as they have disengaged students not showing up to learn.

From my experience in running online programs for students for nearly twenty years, the parameters some school districts outlined to serve students online is nowhere near sufficient for anyone to be successful. Considering the enormous task of large school districts that serve thousands of students, transitioning to an online modality within days isn't realistic, and those that did figure out a system that worked are impressive. What continues to play out in this scenario, however, is the persistent force of the first stage of change: turmoil. These schools are stuck in a vicious cycle of apprehension, fear of the unknown, and loss of control. Schools became apprehensive when they were closed down, and they had to find an alternate modality to reach and support students. Their fear of the unknown pertained to how it would all work and how they would be effective in their roles. They felt a loss of control when they became completely reliant on a system in which they did not feel comfortable or have sufficient experience. As a result, they counted on a system that wasn't effective, and thus all stakeholders lost confidence in the modality as a whole. This pattern is common, and it is where many, if not most, change efforts fail. Without proper planning (in this case, not enough time to plan), an incomplete plan is put into place, and it inevitably fails, resulting in neglect of the initial change that was needed. As a result, there is often a return to the way things have always been done. The challenge in this scenario is that with continued restrictions and concerns of health and safety into the new school year, schools are still faced with the challenge of providing alternative options for students, and the need for change persists. This is where effective planning for change can make a crucial difference.

Proper planning and allotted time to progress through each stage of the change process, including the key emotions within each stage and how individual and collective origins interact with these emotions, is essential in successfully implementing sustainable change. School districts spent the summer planning for the upcoming school year with continued CDC regulations. Surveys were sent out to families to evaluate which learning modality they prefer for the coming school year. Some schools and districts purchased comprehensive online curriculum platforms to offer standard aligned credit-bearing core courses to students to achieve a hybrid approach. Others modified their program to completely online and delivered daily instruction virtually. All of these actions alleviate the perpetual emotions that are created during the initial stage of change.

Leaders during this time can benefit significantly from looking more in-depth at the origins of resistance to this change. What origins of the change are participants being exposed to during this experience that are creating barriers to the change? How might those origins differ among participants, including fellow leaders, teachers, parents, or students? How are the origins of those same participants contributing to the success and progress of the change? How can a leader expand the origins, making positive contributions, and minimize those creating barriers? Time spent looking deeper into resistance to the change that is emerging is well spent as it can address obstacles to successful change and keep them from preventing progression to the next stages of change.

Apprehension, fear of the unknown, and loss of control are all assuaged when these types of planning activities take place. An inventory of preferences, climate surveys, exploration of online solutions, developing scheduling modifications, and communication are all efforts that help transition the change effort to the next stage of grief, which in some ways has been in progress since March when schools initially closed. Their reaction demonstrates the first stage, and planning more effectively for the change may expedite their progression to stage three, commitment, where the stage can be set for more sustainable change, and a new way of educating students could become the norm for schools and districts. As we continue to watch this unfold, planning for key emotions and origin-based responses will remain a critical piece to their overall success.

Stage 2: Regret—Help

The second stage of change is highly personalized and revolves around any type of grief. Everyone grieves in different ways, at different rates, and their grief can vary depending on the depth of the loss, and, of course, our deeply-held origins. Without ample time, care, and support during the grieving process, progression to the next stage of change not only becomes impossible, but may forever deter those to ever be open to the change again, if not given the needed support to rightfully grieve.

Some losses we experience are so traumatic and impactful that we are changed forever and returning to the person we were before the loss isn't always possible. Other changes can be far less compelling, but any type of loss requires ample support to allow for feelings of loss and grieving. Furthermore, personal judgment is important when evaluating just how much time, and support grieving may need. Loss of a close loved one may require an abundance of support, while the time needed to grieve a change to a new curriculum modality may not need as much time or emotional support to adapt.

TRACK/SHIFT Matrix			
	Stage	SHIFT: Leader	
Deconstruct the Old Norm	1	Support	Prepare
			Inform
			Appoint
	2	Help	Counsel
			Organize
			Confirm
Construct the New Norm	3	Imitate	Guide
			Connect
			Persist
	4	Fortify	Invest
			Listen
			Diversify
	5	Transition	Challenge
			Transcend

JessicaSpallino

Table 6.4 SHIFT Stage 2: Help

Grief — Counsel

While losing access to your favorite item at a boutique grocer or experiencing quarantine during a pandemic pales in comparison to losing a loved one, they all involve loss and require us to face change in our lives. We all handle loss in our own ways, and much of that can depend on our deepest origins. My husband thrives on things continuously shifting and almost prefers a fluid environment, where I may react negatively if a plan outdoors gets changed due to the weather. I have observed a variety of responses to loss within my organization and could make educated guesses on those with origins that prefer stability over change. How we approach the differences in capacity for loss can make or break almost any change effort.

It is important to take the time and care to look deeper at individual origins and how they interface with loss because it will impact the amount of support and time needed while grieving. I had a complex relationship with my dad, and when I lost him to suicide it brought up many different emotions aside from sadness and grief. I suffered not only from disorientation and confusion, but also from unresolved feelings and issues I had with him that extended to deep feelings of depression and disconnection from others. After his death, it took me much longer than I expected to function in my life again, and that certainly played a part in my level of accessibility and performance in all areas of my life.

Disorientation — Organize

Any change we experience brings loss, and that loss can generate a state of disorientation until we have become accustomed to the shift. This feeling of disorientation can be a frustrating and challenging time for those who are usually measured, or whose origins led them to prefer to have control over their surroundings. This temporary symptom of change can impact progress and even create doubt that the change holds value or was a good idea in the first place.

Often merged with lingering grief, this sensation requires patience and tolerance to simply be in this, at times, uncomfortable state. Being aware that it is taking place may help, so that harsh judgment from yourself or others doesn't creep in and obstruct this natural stage of the change process. Approaching disorientation with a sense of humor, finding some diversions from the adjustment to change, can ease the pressure and ultimately prevent the development of resistance to the change. This very normal stage of change needs to be approached with a level of lightness and support to allow progress toward the upcoming stages.

Confusion — Confirm

The stage of confusion differs from disorientation. There is a transition from a general feeling that one is in a fog, into an awareness of one's lack of mastery. During this time, behaveiors can become more pointed and, depending on origins at play, can be aggressive enough to modify the trajectory of the change altogether. This final state of the second stage of change as part of the destructing process marks as key in pivoting to the next stages of constructing success for the change. Based on firmly held origins that translate the normal state of confusion during change into a direct sign that the change is not positive or beneficial, change efforts often halt here during this destruction period and never even make it to the upcoming stages of construction.

Addressing confusion during this stage should come with targeted support that eases confusion wherever possible. Synchronization of communication across individuals and groups impacted by the change can be effectively delivered through a variety of communication channels available today and will ease some of the confusion change can bring. Additionally, it can be useful to continuously address how the change will be impacting others as that is usually the biggest concern and where clarity is mostly preferred. Refining elements of the change process such as communication with clarity can be assessed through ongoing one on ones, surveys, and observations during interactions, and improvements can be made as the change process progresses. Being on alert for those active origins during this stage will help alleviate additional pressure and complications during an already potentially trying time.

Leading others during this stage can be a highly interpersonal process and requires ultimate trust and safety between participants. Because loss and grieving are so individual, it requires leaders to not only be as aware as possible of those impacted by loss but how to support them based on their origins. This is not an easy task for any leader, especially if one doesn't hold origins skilled in interpersonal relations. Leaders should commit to working proactively. They must invest time to get to know the individuals with whom they work and become familiar with their origins and tendencies. If a leader is more introverted, they must be sure to make resources available to support those grappling with grief and extended disorientation and confusion. Integrating this into one's leadership practice can benefit everyone greatly when change is enacted, and the channels to support are already cultivated.

The first phase of deconstructing concludes with finding our way through the loss, disorientation, and confusion that change can bring. Once we do this, we can transition to the second phase of constructing within the change process, whether it's the rebuilding of our lives, our organizations, or even something as simple as our daily routine or program we use at work. We will break down those stages and how they all contribute to the phase of constructing during a change in our lives.

Case in Point

Sheryl Sandberg became the first woman to serve on Facebook's board of directors in 2012 and serves as their COO. Before that she was vice president of global online sales and operations at Google, and formerly served as chief of staff for the United States Secretary of the Treasury, Lawrence Summers. She was named on the *Time* 100 annual list of most influential people in the world in 2012, and has authored two books, one of which, *Option B*, is specifically about grief, facing adversity, building resilience, and finding joy.

While on a vacation in Mexico, her husband was found dead near a treadmill in the gym after suffering a cardiac arrhythmia. Sandberg was faced with a traumatic loss and shares in her book her process with loss, grief, and a path through this difficult and sometimes heart-wrenching stage of change. Facing her role as a mother of two young children and a high-profile career while grappling with feelings of loss, disorientation, and confusion was overwhelming, to say the least, but she was eventually able to find some ability to cope with the grief by recognizing that adverse events that create loss or grief aren't personal, pervasive, or permanent. During times of loss and grief, understanding that loss isn't entirely our fault, doesn't impact every aspect of our lives, and won't be a primary focal point forever can liberate us from the pain and unrest that we might feel.

My divorce brought many of these feelings up for me. I was in deep grief over the loss of my marriage and our life together. I wasn't able to focus on life after divorce until I was able to resolve extreme feelings of guilt, failure, and overall grief that plagued for far longer than I imagined. Like Sandberg's reference to her grief and loss as the "elephant in the room" that many friends wouldn't address, I also lost many friends. Some didn't have the ability or interest to ask or talk about the life-changing hardship in my life, and others simply avoided me altogether, likely due to the discomfort it made them feel. This state of disorientation where no one knows exactly how to act or treat one another can amplify the feelings of loss and prolong the grief over what was lost. It can also further trigger more profound confusion about why something so painful and destructive happened to us and how we can recover.

Sandberg talks about what she calls "Option B" — the life that we dig deep to build after a deep loss. Her origins appear to lead her to make sense of things. She recovered as an even more aware person with something to offer to others who may be experiencing something similar. She shed light on the process of grieving and how we can all overcome change I believe my origins may be similar. After a lot of time in the fog of grief, I have dug deep to rebuild a life that is meaningful and fulfilling, and I have attempted to compile my experience to potentially offer any insight I may have to others experiencing something similar.

Phase 2: Constructing the Norm

These last three stages of Commitment, Reinforcement, and Transformation represent the process of constructing the new norm upon the change. Modeling and delivering the means to implement the change is essential during this phase to empower those to evolve into the new norm. As with any construction, developing a strong foundation is critical in making true transformation possible along with close attention to strong origins during these stages.

Stage 3: Action — Imitate

TRACK/SHIFT Matrix			
	Stage	**SHIFT: Leader**	
Deconstruct the Old Norm	1	Support	Prepare
			Inform
			Appoint
	2	Help	Counsel
			Organize
			Confirm
Construct the New Norm	3	Imitate	Guide
			Connect
			Persist
	4	Fortify	Invest
			Listen
			Diversify
	5	Transition	Challenge
			Transcend

JessicaSpallino

Table 6.5 SHIFT Stage 3: Imitate

The third stage marks the initial step in constructing the foundation for the change. With much of the turmoil and grieving dealt with during the first phase of the change process, modeling initial elements of the new norm for others impacted by the change to emulate is critical. Informed confidence is essential to demonstrate during this phase as work toward establishing the new norm takes place. Without a vision, communication, and tenacity, change efforts may halt here, and the hard work completed during the first two stages may never be fully actualized.

Vision — Guide

The first step in modeling a new norm for change during the construction phase is developing a vision. Pursuing change without a clear vision that creates an overall goal can create little chance for it to come to fruition. Developing purpose individually or collectively generates a level of investment that can dominate the trials and tribulations that change can inevitably bring. A vision can incite inspiration when the mechanics and challenges of change impact those working toward it. Ensuring the development of vision includes a holistic view of the change, the purpose behind the change, and making sure that it encompasses all those that will be impacted by the change are all critical to managing successful change.

In many circumstances, it is useful to recruit others to help develop a vision so that it includes perspectives that may be overlooked by a singular leader. In more personal cases, the development of the vision should closely align to the overall purpose and intent of the vision guiding the change. An effective vision can often act as a wise grandparent. When you fall off a path and are unsure of which direction to go, a good talk with a grandparent can often put things in perspective and remind you not only of who you are and capable of, but what you are striving toward. Similarly, a vision works in that it can create a general path to achieve your overall goal. If you are thrown off that path due to infinite challenging factors, it can be easily revisited and given a refreshment of perspective and remind you what you are working toward.

Communication — Connect

Communication is key in ensuring everyone involved during change is informed throughout the process. Keeping in touch with those impacted by the change helps prevent many challenging emotions that may emerge, such as fear of the unknown and losing control. The more informed change participants are, the higher the chance the change will be successful.

Any change should be accompanied by ample communication — ideally proactive communication, rather than reactive. Within organizations, the increased efforts at communication can start before the change plan has even been decided. Ideally, ideas for change can be shared with the people it will impact before it begins and as it is still being explored as a way to make sure they have the opportunity to provide feedback and to help shape how the change may look. Once a final decision has been made, it is important to map out the specifics — the who, what, when, where, and why — and provide updates in these areas regularly. Changes that are made within the change plan — and there will likely be many — are essential to share before the participants stumble across the change in plans themselves. Developing trust that things will take place in the way you have said they will is vital to keeping everyone invested and supportive of the change.

Tenacity — Persist

It is a natural tendency to default to the norm before a change has been fully implemented. If any challenges come up throughout the change, and without any doubt there will be, the magnetic force to the old way of doing something will prevail, and the attempted change will simply become a distant memory. I have observed in my organization and many others how a change starts, but then falls victim to the claws of stagnation once any challenge surfaces. Obstacles to the change can range from a variety of sources such as lack of funding, loss of interest or motivation, gains in change opposition momentum, the change no longer being needed, not enough human capital to assist in the implementation, not enough time, misalignment to the overall goal, and likely many others.

We all have likely had first-hand experience with at least one of the challenges listed here during change, and though most are not easy to overcome, they all are often within our power to overcome. Ensuring that the change is needed and aligns with that ever-so-important vision should be accomplished in the initial steps of identifying and planning needed change. The rest of the challenges, no matter how insurmountable they seem, can be overcome by our equally powerful natural propensity for tenacity. Change without perseverance is like trying to throw a ball without the force your arm generates. There is no change without persistence—they go hand in hand, like any dynamic duo. When the change process takes some blows, it requires our innate tenaciousness to see it through. Those selected to be most instrumental in moving the change along should hold deep origins of tenacity and strong will and this will be easy to identify for those leaders that continuously familiarize themselves with the deep origins of others.

Case in Point

After graduating college and working at a ski lodge for a year, Howard Shultz started his career as a salesman for Xerox. He went on to become a general manager for a Swedish kitchenware manufacturer, where he led the coffee machine manufacturer operations in the U.S. While in that role, he visited the Starbucks Coffee Company in Seattle, Washington to fulfill their plastic cone filter orders. One year later, he was hired as director of retail operations and marketing for Starbucks. After a trip to Milan, Italy, he was inspired by the espresso experience and tried to convince the owners to integrate espresso beverages into their menu. They tried the concept, and though it was successful, they weren't willing to take it on permanently, as they felt too unfamiliar with the concept and logistics. His vision firmly intact, Shultz left to start his own espresso beverage business, Il Giornale, and needed $400,000 in startup capital. He was able to raise $150,000 from one of the Starbucks owners, another $100,000 from a local doctor, and the rest from 25 of the 242 investors he approached.

Two years later, the original Starbucks team sold its retail unit to Shultz to further pursue Peet's Coffee & Tea. Shultz expanded Starbucks' reach across the U.S. and maintained ownership of every store, becoming widely known for introducing and solidifying the coffee culture in the U.S. In 1992, Starbucks had its initial public offering, raising $271 million, which allowed them to double their number of stores. Shultz spent the following years expanding throughout China and made improvements toward employee conditions and benefits, including the Starbucks College Achievement Plan, which supports employee's college tuition. He also enforced the company's fair trade and ethical source policies for their coffee bean supply chain in Africa and other coffee-producing countries. He doubled the company's annual purchase of fair trade coffee.

Shultz oversaw growth from 11 Seattle coffeehouses in Seattle to 28,000 stores in 77 countries and contributed nearly $100 billion to the company's market capitalizations. In 2018, he stepped down from active management.

Shultz's Starbucks venture is an excellent demonstration not only of his origins in action, but of his progression as a leader through the three elements of this stage of change: developing a vision, communication, and tenacity. While constructing this disruption to the coffee industry, Shultz developed an idea for the new business he wanted to pursue. He tested it out with his first opening, addressed any issues within it, and refined it to ensure that it was one that was not just inspiring, but achievable as well. Upon polishing and finalizing the vision for his venture, he combined the two elements of this change stage — communication and tenacity — to find funding for the new business. His tenacious origins led him to communicate to anyone he thought might be interested. After pitching his idea to over 200 people, he was able to secure the initial funding for his project.

Additionally, when the Starbucks management team lost sight of the vision for Starbucks and decided to pursue another coffee venture, Schultz stuck to his well-developed vision and his innate tenacity. He doubled its exposure by raising nearly $3 million and dominating the coffee culture in the U.S.

Shultz's progression through the third stage of change is a great model to reference when planning for the first stage of constructing change. The critical need for a well-developed vision, supported by inspiration and passion is vital in generating buy-in and investment in the proposed change. Communicating the inspired change is essential to ensure clarity of the change, and ongoing investment takes place. Shultz communicated and executed his vision into the growth of his stores and culture throughout the U.S. and beyond. Change attempts can often never materialize due to the endless obstacles that can interrupt progress. The utmost tenacity can very often be required to see change through, and Shultz demonstrates that every step of the way during the major disruption he delivered to the coffee industry.

Stage 4: Completion — Fortify

As part of the continued efforts to construct change, the fourth stage of change, Reinforcement, is where specific elements of the change are delivered. Assuming that a foundation has been fortified with a solid vision supported by continuous communication, this stage extends into specialized aspects of the change. It allows for enhancement through personal expression and support. This stage relies heavily on familiarity with the origins of those impacted by the change as it calls for the empowerment, individualization, and creativity that can be expressed during this lighter, more personal, yet equally important stage of change.

Empowerment — Invest

Empowerment is critical during a change to ensure investment for all involved in the change. Empowerment can transition change efforts from being merely tolerated to creating

	Stage	SHIFT: Leader	
TRACK/SHIFT Matrix			
Deconstruct the Old Norm	1	Support	Prepare
			Inform
			Appoint
	2	Help	Counsel
			Organize
			Confirm
Construct the New Norm	3	Imitate	Guide
			Connect
			Persist
	4	Fortify	Invest
			Listen
			Diversify
	5	Transition	Challenge
			Transcend

JessicaSpallino

Table 6.6 SHIFT Stage 4: Fortify

active participants and promoters who equally care about its success as those who initiated the change. Often those that initiate change hold deep origins that fuel it, whether it is passionate drive and tenacity or a deep emotional connection to the change they are pursuing. Much of their empowerment is innate, or events in their lives trigger it; they have the ambition to initiate and devote themselves to the change. For the change to maintain a trajectory for success, the empowerment of others becomes necessary to help see the change through and convince others of its value. Often during change efforts, neutrality about the change is rare. Most are either for the change or against it, and empowering others to care about the change and to be part of it is crucial.

People who are positively invested in the change not only can contribute to its success, but through their commitment to it, they can recruit others on to the change bandwagon. For this kind of commitment to manifest, the change must hold value for others, it must solve a problem, or address a pain point they are experiencing. Once the change has been thoroughly tested for relevancy, which should take place during previous stages, then the work continues in the area of building reinforcement through empowering those involved in the change. A leader makes this possible by being attentive to the participant's position. They must also be aware of people's origins, which influence the way they interact with the change. Those who support the change can be further empowered through the assignment of direct initiatives within the change and help others who are undecided to see the value of the change and how it can positively impact them. Working with people who are against the change is where much of the challenging work lies. It is essential to ensure that the vision of the change and how it affects them is reiterated throughout the process so that the solution is continuously and easily visible. For those deeply resistant, regular one-on-ones can help to provide a place for them to discuss their anxieties and concerns along with expectations of their involvement. Doing this can nudge them along in a supportive and caring way. It may be unrealistic to assume that every participant will be accessible to empower during the change process, but it is important to try where possible and rely on those that are in support of it.

Individualization — Listen

Expecting that all change agents and participants will handle change the same way and contribute equally is not realistic or practical. Anyone leading an organization or who has more than one child can attest to the high variance of individual tendencies, tolerances, and personalities coexisting within one unit. Taking the time and care to nurture individual differences can be a worthwhile investment during change, and anytime for that matter. When support is personalized to the needs of the individual, their unique strengths are encouraged and can flourish and ultimately contribute to the change like no other can.

Though as a parent, leader of an organization, change participant, or change agent, accommodating others with multiple and at times extreme styles and preferences can be tedious and time-consuming, it can also be thoroughly rewarding for the family, organization, the change, and of course, the individual. Committing to not only support but reinforce individual strengths can create high performers during change as contributions become highly unique and specialized. Without the encouragement of individuality, we'd likely have no change, innovations, or novel solutions at all. Helping others connect to their strengths can create an incredibly dynamic and effective organization with new solutions to problems on an ongoing basis. As a leader, this requires getting to know each and everyone with which you work through one-on-ones, inventories, surveys, and continuous observations. Supporting self-exploration in an infinitely safe environment, where others feel entirely safe to not only be themselves, but take continual risks and even fail is essential in maximizing everyone's strengths. The process of individualizing support recognizes areas for growth within each person. Providing a safe arena to openly address deficiencies can be just as important as supporting strengths. This stage is where active listening and a coaching approach with others can help address both strengths and areas for growth in an ongoing, safe, and constructive environment. Developing a culture of safety might be the best thing any leader can do in creating a dynamic and solutions-based environment.

Creativity — Diversity

In addition to supporting and encouraging the development of individual strengths, allowing the space and freedom for creative expression during the change process can help to deepen investment and ownership, furthering the development of the change in innovative ways and making it a light and enjoyable stage of the process. After the deep and challenging work toward the change has been accomplished, some time is needed to let go of fear and to add personal flair to the change. My co-founder has a marketing background and has a very fluid approach to his work as far as changing themes, messaging, and graphics within the marketing for our organization. He is given the ultimate freedom to experiment and express himself creatively within the marketing initiatives and this has allowed for creative and innovative ways to communicate our brand to others. This level of afforded creativity has helped to promote a brand that differentiates ourselves from our competitors and offer truly unique branding experiences from a TV channel within our platform that delivers news within our community to a graphic novel themed campaign geared towards students. This opportunity for creativity can make for a far more exciting and personally reflective implementation that others will likely enjoy and remember.

Writing this book was not only a therapeutic process for me, but a creative endeavor that encompasses and represents a lifetime of grueling, and, at times, enjoyable change — for me, sharing my experiences and perspectives culminated in a book to share with others. It could have been a song if I were a musician, a painting if I was an artist, or a polished website if I was a website designer. Finding the creative expressive means, whatever that looks like, can be extremely therapeutic for others who have gone through a change. However small, it can also contribute to the change in constructive and fulfilling ways. Creative contributions to a new change implementtation add color and personality to a new normal that can delight and impress others involved in and utilizing the change. As a leader, referring to the ongoing inventories and knowledge you have on others impacted by the change informs how to encourage a creative outlet during this time in the change process and apply their personal stamp on the change that they helped make possible. Being as open as possible to the creative way others may express themselves at this time helps in furthering the safe and individualized culture needed during the change process.

Case in Point

Robyn Rihanna Fenty was born in Saint Michael, Barbados, and grew up listening to reggae and hip-hop music. She was subject to an abusive home due to her father's alcoholism and crack cocaine addiction and would try to get in between her mother and father during fights and physical abuse. In 2003, she formed a musical trio with two classmates. She was discovered as an individual talent by an American record producer in Barbados and was signed to a production company shortly after. Rihanna has gone on to sell over 250 million records, earned 14 number-one singles, 31 top-ten singles in the U.S., and 30 top-ten entries in the UK. She has been awarded nine Grammy Awards, 13 American Music Awards, 12 Billboard Music Awards, and six Guinness World Records. She was ranked one of the top ten highest-paid celebrities by *Forbes* in 2012 and 2014, is the wealthiest female musician with an estimated net worth of $600 million, and was named one of the most 100 most influential people in the world in 2012 and 2018.

We may primarily know Rihanna as a hugely successful singer, songwriter, and performer, but she has also accomplished incredible breakthroughs in a variety of influential areas where she achieved genuine change. She developed a deep interest in fashion and was drawn to the power that style had in amplifying her mark beyond the music world. Through her empowerment as an icon and established influence in the music world, she began creatively expressing herself in the fashion world in unique and dramatic ways that eventually led to her being given the fashion icon award of the year in 2014 by the Council of Fashion Designers of America. Rihanna became the first black brand ambassador for Dior in 2015. From there, she became creative director for Puma, and she started her own active wear brand in 2014 while she was simultaneously working for both Puma's owner, Kering, and its rival, Louis Vuitton (LVMH), which was unprecedented and was a testament to her unique power and brand in the market. She later developed her own lingerie company that included styles for diverse body types and colors, and then developed a makeup line that specialized in products for all kinds of skin types and tones.

Most groundbreaking of all is Rihanna's fashion line under LVMH, marking her as the first woman and black person to achieve such an arrangement. Celled Fenty, the brand launched in 2019, and includes clothing, accessories, and footwear, and was the first new brand launch for LVMH since 1987. With no artistic limits, this collaboration stands as one of the most visible demonstrations of the power that celebrity and social media influencers have on brands reaching their potential audiences. Rihanna utilized her public persona and fierce individual creativity to achieve this. Not only has this landed her great success, but it has paved a path for future opportunities as well. The Government of Barbados appointed her as ambassador devoted to promoting education, tourism, and investment. Rihanna also founded the nonprofit organization Clara Lionel Foundation, which provides funds for breakthrough education endeavors and emergency preparedness and response programs around the world. In 2020, her foundation pledged $5 million to support families impacted by the COVID-19 pandemic in a combined effort with Jay Z-s foundation and Jack Dorsey, of CEO of Twitter and Square, to get tests and medical supplies to Haiti and Malawi.

Rihanna's origins provided her with boldness, empowerment, individuality, and creativity, which allowed her to build a tremendous career and have positive influence in a variety of areas. She has served as an influential leader in the music and fashion industry and has made significant strides in her philanthropic work within her communities and throughout the world. She is a role model for so many, and she exemplifies how to empower yourself to make a difference. Rihanna shows us how to rely on our innate individuality and creative expression to impact change, not only in our own lives, but throughout the world.

Stage 5: Keep — Transform

TRACK/SHIFT Matrix			
	Stage	**SHIFT: Leader**	
Deconstruct the Old Norm	1	Support	Prepare
			Inform
			Appoint
	2	Help	Counsel
			Organize
			Confirm
Construct the New Norm	3	Imitate	Guide
			Connect
			Persist
	4	Fortify	Invest
			Listen
			Diversify
	5	Transition	Challenge
			Transcend

Table 6.7 SHIFT Stage 5: Transition

This final stage of a change effort, Transformation, is the key to making the change sustainable. Once much of the construction of the change is accomplished, it is essential to ensure that the new norm is established and a transition in behavior and mindset are in place. Without this transformation of expectations, beliefs, and actions, every change runs the risk of defaulting back to the way things were previously done. It is a natural tendency of ours to return to what is familiar and ingrained, so this last stage is critical in ensuring a real transformation to live and be the change.

Revolutionize — Challenge

Change can be difficult to attain with so many obstacles and resistances that, when and if achieved, it can be quite revolutionary. The ability to extricate oneself, and especially others, from the way things have always been done is no small feat. Within voluntary change, it must be solving a problem or pain point to take hold and make an impact. It needs to be convincing that it is worthwhile and will make life easier, better, and more fulfilling. Though some changes are minor and less impactful, such as trying a new shampoo or getting a new phone, others are more revolutionary in that they are oppositional to deeply held origins, such as igniting police reform or learning online.

Change requires vision, communication, and tenacity to challenge rooted origins of resistance. Revolutionary change certainly requires these three things but is combined with a level of boldness that drives the change and aims to dismantle old ways of thinking and doing things. This level of courage is what makes any dynamic and difficult change possible. Tapping into this boldness and helping to cultivate it in others is an art form. Some may hold origins in this area, and enacting revolutionary change seems to be somewhat natural.

In contrast, others develop an intense drive, tackling their counter origins and those in others to make significant change happen. Becoming familiar with where we lie on that spectrum can help inform the direct actions to take in ourselves and with others. Supporting ourselves and others in deconstructing the obstacles that lie within us and around us is vital in making revolutionary change happen. Committing to discovering where the obstacles lie and addressing them on an individual and collective basis requires patience, courage, and understanding to achieve the most purposeful change. The more we incorporate this into our change practice, the more likely meaningful change can happen.

Evolve — Transcend

Once a change is fully implemented, and it has progressed through each stage, the new norm takes the place of the old one. Our evolution becomes evident when we find ourselves entertained by the ways we used to do things. "Remember when we used to print out directions to bring with us to know how to get somewhere new?" or "Can you believe we used to have to flip open our phones to use them?" After working tirelessly through the demanding stages of change, this is where it becomes the new norm, and a genuine detachment from the old norm is solidified. It may seem miraculous, but when the change is one that solves a problem or pain point, like the pain of having to print out directions before your travels, it happens.

Evolution is a result of the culmination of many steps and essential elements that we've explored throughout the change process. Like training for a marathon, once those steps have been thoroughly completed, performing in the race in on. If the work throughout the stages has been tended to with ample care and investment, this final stage can happen more naturally than any of the other stages. If it needs a little help along the way, it can involve further reinforcement and support in areas showing signs of reluctance, which can be monitored through ongoing surveys, evaluations, and observations. Areas needing additional work can often be infrastructure development, refined processes and systems, additional training, and targeted coaching for those with deeply held resistant origins. Once the stage is further set for true transformation, the work is far from over. Because change is constant, observing and evaluating for modifications needed to be made to the change or the need for altogether new changes will always be required to remain relevant, effective, and in solution development mode, so the task of evolving is ever-present.

Case in Point

Frederick Smith was born in Mississippi in 1944. He was crippled as a child from a bone disease until his recovery by age ten. He developed a passion for flying as a child and became an amateur pilot when he was a teenager. He attended Yale, where he earned a degree in Economics and was friends with both George W. Bush and John Kerry. He wrote a paper for an Economics course about an idea he had for an overnight delivery service that would utilize advanced technology. His professor wasn't very impressed and suggested that in order for him to receive a grade higher than a C for the paper, the plan had to be attainable. This paper became the idea for Smith's future overnight delivery empire, FedEx.

After graduating from college, Smith was commissioned in the U.S. Marine Corps and served for three years, where he served as a platoon leader and trained to fly with pilots to observe and control ground action. He served two tours of duty in Vietnam and flew on over 200 combat missions. He received the Silver Star for capturing two hostile soldiers and numerous valuable documents and equipment and was discharged in 1969. In 1970, Smith purchased the controlling interest in an aircraft maintenance company and transitioned its focus to trading used jets. In June of 1971, Smooth founded FedEx with $4 million in inheritance and raised an additional $91 million in venture capital to serve 25 cities with small packages and documents. He developed the first integrated air-ground system where one shipment center was located in the middle of the representative shipment centers, and all their representatives were sent to the central location to exchange shipments. In the very early days, after a critically needed loan was denied, Smith took the company's last $5,000 to Vegas and won $27,000 on blackjack to pay for their fuel bill, buying another week of survival.

Smith also co-owns the NFL's Washington Football Team and several entertainment companies. He was offered the position of Defense Secretary twice during George W. Bush's presidential term, but due to medical reasons and later to be with his terminally ill daughter, he declined. He served on John McCain's campaign committee as National Co-Chairman. Smith has earned multiple awards and honors throughout the years, including the Tony Jannus Award for his distinguished contributions to commercial aviation and in 2011, and was ranked the 26th of the World's Greatest Leaders by *Fortune* magazine.

Smith relied heavily on his origins to develop a world-changing industry of overnight delivery. FedEx has revolutionized how businesses and individuals alike conduct business, and we have transformed into a society where life without it is hardly imaginable. As displayed in his childhood as a boy overcoming his handicap or earning a Silver Star in the Marine Corps as a young adult, Smith's origins in boldness, tenacity, and passion for aviation not only changed an entire shipping industry, but continues to disrupt it. His perseverance and leadership skills have brought FedEx success for over 40 years, and he continuously informs the industry's capabilities through improvements such as online package tracking. FedEx currently employs nearly 300,000 people and remains a brilliant model for transformation within an industry during change.

Reflection

> Consider an experience you've had with any category of change adopter and the actions you employed to support that person in maintaining the change at hand. What worked well in supporting that person? What wasn't as effective? Do any of the SHIFT actions seem like they may have helped in that particular situation? Why or why not?

Chapter 7: Planning for Change

Planning for change is the key tool a leader can use that to successfully implement change. Ensuring that there is a developed plan to navigate through the TRACK stages of change for the participant and the SHIFT stages of change as a leader can help with the varying change adopter levels and ORs they bring to the change process.

	Stage	TRACK: Participant		SHIFT: Leader	
			TRACK/SHIFT Matrix		
Deconstruct the Old Norm	1	Turmoil	Apprehension	Support	Prepare
			Fear of the Unknown		Inform
			Loss of Control		Appoint
	2	Regret	Grief	Help	Counsel
			Disorientation		Organize
			Confusion		Confirm
Construct the New Norm	3	Adjustment	Vision	Imitate	Guide
			Communication		Connect
			Tenacity		Persist
	4	Commitment	Empowerment	Fortify	Invest
			Individualization		Listen
			Creativity		Diversify
	5	Keep	Revolutionize	Transition	Challenge
			Evolve		Transcend

JessicaSpallino

Table 7.1 TRACK/SHIFT Matrix

We have explored the stages of TRACK from a participant perspective and we have reviewed a variety of leadership scenarios demonstrating an array of origins that have contributed towards enacted change. Each scenario offers a glimpse into some of the dynamic origins at play as well as the planning required to overcome obstacles and achieve successful change. Many of the change leaders we've discussed demonstrate at least one of the stages of SHIFT, as outlined below.

For example, Howard Shultz of Starbucks and Fred Smith of FedEx pursued their visions of espresso stocked coffee houses and overnight delivery with an intense persistence, regardless of the obstacles they were consistently presented and ultimately revolutionized the industries in which they contributed. Rhianna diversified her musical performer status to that of savvy and creative fashion icon, becoming the first black woman to master a monumental business arrangement with world leader in luxury goods, Louis Vuitton.

Changes we champion in our everyday lives may not make the news headlines or be billion dollar business ventures, but they can be relatively challenging and planning for the SHIFT stages of leading through change can make them possible and ultimately successful. Any change we pursue is vulnerable to the array of change adopters involved in the change process and if not addressed and prepared for, can deter change from materializing.

Change Adopters at Change Organization			
Role	Adopter Trait	Needed Action to Support	Change Org Member
Leader	Leading the change	- Plan	Co-Founder 1
Change Agent	Initiates the Change	- Research - Share	Myself (Lead Team)
Implementors	Administer directive and oversee change	- Prepare - Inform - Appoint - Invest - Listen - Diversify	Myself Teachers
Supporters	Compliant and buy-in to the change	- Counsel - Organize - Confirm - Invest - Listen - Diversify	Co-Founder 1 Business Manager Teachers Group 1
Resistors	Resistant to the change	- Guide - Connect - Persist	Lead Team Teachers Group 2
Defiants	Oppose the change	- Listen - Diversify - Challenge - Transcend	Co-Founder 2 Lead Team

Table 7.2 Change Adopters at Change Organization

The example of my experience during change as the change agent within my previous organization (Change Organization) devastated by destructive ORs, offers a lucid example of how important planning for change can be. After much reflection and the development of the TRACK and SHIFT stages of change, I believe the lack of planning through the stages during the changes I pursued is the primary cause of the change not being successful and the overall destruction within the organization. Consideration and preparation for the change adopters' ORs through the stages of change may have positively impacted the change efforts and avoided the contention it helped to create. To demonstrate the importance of planning for the ORs of the change adopters through the stages of change, I've outlined the change adopters' roles involved in the change within Change Organization in Table 10.2

When applying the TRACK and SHIFT stages to my tumultuous change experience at Change Organization, it becomes quite easy to identify where and why the breakdowns took place. The attempted change got derailed by destructive origins of change resistance without the proper leadership and planning. Any change requires effective leadership, planning and consideration of the deep and volatile origins at play during change.

To prevent the damage that transpired at Change Organization, the primary leader needed to have planned for the change process more effectively. Having a better understanding and knowledge of the participants' origins and supporting them through those origins may have kept some of the destructive behavior from thriving. As the leader, achieving the delicate balance between imposing professional and collaborative expectations along with ongoing support for the lead team's origins may have helped ease their anxieties and deep fear of the unknown. Because this didn't effectively take place, the change process halted in the first two stages of change, Turmoil and Regret. Enforcing expectations along with providing support would have helped every category of change adopters at Change Organization, and could have prevented those that became defiants from doing so. Because ample planning and care for resistant origins didn't take place, the resistors transitioned to defiants. Once that took place, there was nothing else left to do but either let them go or allow them to make the decision to do so, which they eventually did.

	Leadership Plan for SHIFT at Change Organization	
Support	Prepare	- Identify and openly discuss need for change first with lead team, then with all participants - Consider all ideas/input
	Inform	- Share potential implementations first with lead team, then with all - Refine implementation based on feedback
	Appoint	- Assign implementation duties to lead team and participants - Allow and include modifications based on participant feedback
Help	Counsel	- Conduct ongoing 1/1s to help counsel the resisters and defiants with resistant ORs - Combine enforced expectations with empathetic tolerance
	Organize	- Execute plans systematically for all - Ensure implementation aligns to expectations as closely as possible
	Confirm	- Reiterate need for change to all - Articulate the solution the implementation is providing amongst any uncertainty
Imitate	Guide	- Provide a well-developed vision for the change and how it to aligns to org's outcomes - Ensure participation and buy-in to vision from as many participants as possible
	Connect	- Conduct regular briefings and check-ins to develop transparency and investment from all participants - Meet more regularly with those showing signs of struggle- resisters and defiants
	Persist	- Apply consistent expectations of change duties with all participants - Continue to counsel resisters and defiants, maintaining accountability
Fortify	Invest	- Take the time to inventory perception and climate of all participants - Apply extra care where needed
	Listen	- Develop coaching system to ensure all participants are being heard and considered - Generate actions where needed
	Diversify	- Individualize support and accommodations - Allow creative adaptations to implementation to foster investment and buy-in
Transition	Challenge	- Call on all participants to elevate the organization to a level of improvement through innovation and change - Model and expect full embrace of the change with the old norm as a reflection
	Transcend	- Model and guide organization in the new norm - Recruit others to develop ways to build upon the new norm for continuous change and improvement

Table 7.3 Leadership Plan for SHIFT at Change Organization

As the primary Change Agent and Implementor there, I also could have helped to prevent some of the damage if I had planned for the change more effectively. I would have been far more successful if I had taken the time to plan out the research for my proposed changes and shared that research on a regular basis with the key leadership and staff there. If I had appointed more of the lead team and teachers to help with the implementation tasks, they may have invested in the change and supported its delivery. If I had exercised the care to listen to their feedback and diversify the change plans to reflect their contributions, they may have bought in to the change. Compromises sometimes need to be made with all the participants to ensure the change reflects the opinions and needs of all those it will impact. To overlook the feedback and requests of change participants puts the change at risk from actualizing. My experience at Change Organization is a concrete example of how much damage neglecting these actions can create.

Throughout the change process at Change Organization, I demonstrated the same intensity I saw in my dad growing up when he fought for what he believed was right. He sometimes became so committed to the fight that he wasn't able to see the opposing viewpoint or the bigger picture. This similar origin of mine caused me to do the same during this fight for change. I became so devoted to the fight for what I thought was right, that I neglected to consider the resistors' perspectives or the bigger picture of what was right for the overall organization. This change experience has become a significant opportunity for me to address this origin of mine to prevent the damage it can create in all areas of my life.

If I was afforded the opportunity go back and try to make the attempted change right, I'd offer the introduction in Table 10.3 to a plan that may have salvaged the efforts and better managed the ORs of all involved in the attempted change at Change Organization.

Based on applying the SHIFT stages to the change at Change Organization, many critical steps throughout the change process could have been taken to minimize the turmoil and potentially ensure change success. Allowing time and care for each stage is imperative to see a change process through to the end of transcendence from the old norm. Because this didn't take place from the leadership at Change Organization, the change stalled in the first two stages. The change never fully made it to the next phase of constructing the new norm and its corresponding stages of Adjustment, Commitment and Keep. Though still just an outline for a change plan, it commits devotion to each stage, change adopter category and possible ORs they may each bring.

For example, if during the first stage of Support, open discussions identifying the need for the change and true consideration of all ideas and input were more respectfully considered, the participants may not have started to resist as strongly as they did. And if during the

Help stage the execution of systematic plans for all participants was more organized and communicated, the resistors may not have started to organize themselves to try and overturn the change. The neglect of change planning in alignment to the TRACK and SHIFT stages of change, increases the propensity for a change adopter of any category to eventually resist and ultimately become a destructive defiant. Inversely, the more we apply the actions of SHIFT as a leader during change, the less likely participants will become defiants in the illustration below.

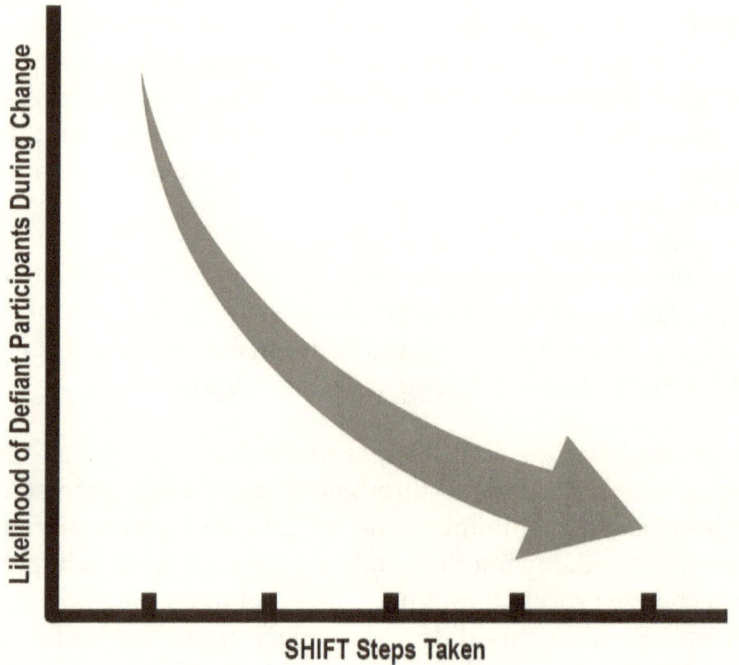

Table 7.4 Leadership Plan for SHIFT at Change Organization

Preventing any change participants from starting out as defiants or becoming defiants during change is impossible. Some participants possess defiant origins that will not be accessible to change. If these defiants are not addressed by effective leadership, they can destroy not only the change, but the overall culture of the organization. Utilizing the SHIFT actions wherever possible and maintaining awareness as a leader are both key in monitoring the presence of defiants throughout the change process.

Return to the example of a change to a flight plan on a plane. If the leaders (pilots) and implementors (flight crew) provide ample planning and communication to all of the change participants (passengers), there is less of a chance that some may become hysterical defiants and need to be detained. The more the plan is shared with accommodations for those with any concern, the less likely there will be resistors and defiants. The ample planning and communication as part of the SHIFT stages of action, treat origins that may be at play in any of the participants and can avoid destructive behavior that leads to destructive behavior of resistors and defiants. It is important to note that some resistors or defiants will not be able to be swayed to a more change friendly category. This is why effective leadership skills and background knowledge of participant's origins through proactive daily practice, makes a critical difference. Familiarity with the origins of a leader's change participants can determine whether the change survives the usual resistance and eventually becomes the new norm, or if it never even makes it through each stage and halts the destruction of the old norm.

This book aims to provide a clear foundation for the theory that combines the consideration of origins and effective leadership to enact change. TRACK identifies the participant's stages through change, while SHIFT provides actions leaders can take to support participants through those change stages. The next step to complete the theory is the planning for change. The process of planning for change will be more clearly defined in a sequel to this book. From a leader perspective during a change effort, further details of each stage will be more clearly defined as part of an overall systematic plan for change.

Considering the variety of origins at play during any change, care and preparedness for those origins throughout a change plan are critical for the success of anyone pursuing the fulfilling task of enacting change. I sincerely hope you will join me on the next step to accomplish meaningful change through effective planning and always looking deeper.

Epilogue

When I think of change, I think of the leaves changing colors in the fall, or my puppy tripling his size in less than a year. I also think of my parents and grandparents that I've lost, and life after divorce. Change is necessary in all ways and though brutally painful at times, it is how we grow, evolve, and develop new paths in our lives. Not only is change necessary, but it is needed in a variety of social and political ways, and depending on who you talk to, those ways differ. I write this not only during the COVID-19 pandemic, but once we started to see a plateau in outbreaks, social protests erupted due to police aggression and the recorded murder of a black man being apprehending with a knee in his neck during a potential arrest. The recording shows George Floyd pleading for his life, stating, "I can't breathe," and after over eight minutes, he eventually dies. During a time of continued grief over a major and unprecedented disruption to our lives, came the loss of life due to a tragic event displaying the roots and origins of racism.

What followed were protests in remarkable numbers across the country and even in places throughout the world, in support of Black Lives Matter, a continued organized movement advocating against police brutality against black people. This upheaval in social justice, the closure of businesses due to the pandemic, the backlash against wearing facial masks, and the looting of fragile businesses that opted to open created a collision in origins that run so deep, that a workable solution or compromise just doesn't seem attainable. The climate in our communities and the entire country is afflicted with grief and turmoil, and the more we try to move forward, the more entangled in opposition we become.

In observing this time of heightened unrest, it is not difficult to see deep origins of resistance in many facets of our society. The COVID-19 pandemic has brought unprecedented levels of fear, uncertainty, loss, grief, disorientation, confusion, and restlessness for many people. These symptoms and steps of change all reflect the first phase of change as they include the destruction of norms on a widespread basis, and all of the younger generations during this time have no experience with such a dismantling of normal expectations. Combined with continued turmoil and grief, we are struggling to transition to the second phase of change, where the construction of new norms begins to take place. Fragmented and politically-charged federal and local leadership, development time for a vaccine, a deeply impacted economy, and overall restlessness and confusion are all barriers to the country moving on to the next stages of change where we commit, reinforce and transform. As we started to develop a vision for what things might look and how to develop a new norm, the protests erupted, and our attention swayed. As we began to witness a plateau in COVID-19 cases and businesses began to open with new rules established, the stage of reinforcement was diverted. We are currently experiencing a spike in cases and a pause in reopening many businesses, which is creating somewhat of a halt in the change process.

As with any change, however painful and unprecedented, its ultimate success and sustainability rely on what research has found to be the most critical factor: leadership. Our ability to reach the next stage of change ultimately depends on our leadership, from the very top of the country, to the leader within each household. Leadership within the government, whose sole purpose is to serve its people, is where much power to currently change lies. The power lies within leadership at the state, county, and city level, within influential businesses and organizations and schools and school districts and every community and home. Much of that leadership is polarized and unable to bring us all together to solve these problems and transform them in a unified way. The obstacle to making this happen is origins. Origins at play within every level of leadership are keeping our communities and the entire country from progressing through change.

It is inspiring to envision what could happen if individuals and entire bodies of government had the insight and courage to look deeper at resistant origins within themselves and their supporting constituents and worked to dissolve them for the greater good. It is hopeful to imagine influential businesses and organizations, including school districts, addressing contentious origins, preventing change for the good of all people of our communities. What could happen if each of us went about our daily lives—standing six feet apart, wearing masks while standing in the line at the supermarket—paid attention to those origins within each one of us? What keeps us from behaving like a community interested in and committed to problem-solving and inclusive vision building? What could happen if we all resolve some of our deepest, most adversarial origins to meet in the middle and continue to create a world we were born to contribute to and appreciate? What origins did impactful leaders such as Abraham Lincoln, Mohandas Gandhi, Martin Luther King, Malala Yousafzazi, Nelson Mandela, and Angela Merkel have to face within themselves and their communities to make change possible? How difficult and unprecedented were the times and climate they were facing, and most importantly, how did they lead others, with varying origins, through change?

List of Tables

Table 1.1 Central Themes and Statements Regarding Educators' Response to Change

Table 1.2 Clusters and Themes Regarding Educator's Response to Change

Table 1.3 Clusters, Themes, and Identifiers Regarding Educator's Response to Change

Table 1.4 Key Findings based on Clusters, Themes, and Identifiers Regarding Educator's Response to Change

Table 2.1 Change Adopter Categories

Table 2.2 TRACK Stages

Table 2.3 TRACK/SHIFT Matrix

Table 3.1 Stage 1: Turmoil

Table 3.2 Stage 2: Regret

Table 4.1 Stage 3: Adjustment

Table 4.2 Stage 4: Commitment

Table 4.3 Change Adopters Within My Family

Table 4.4 Change Adopters at My Previous Organization

Table 4.5 Stage 5: Keep

Table 6.1 TRACK/SHIFT Matrix

Table 6.2 Supportive Actions for Change Adopters

Table 6.3 SHIFT Stage 1: Support

Table 6.4 SHIFT Stage 2: Help

Table 6.5 SHIFT Stage 3: Imitate

Table 6.6 SHIFT Stage 4: Fortify

Table 6.7 SHIFT Stage 5: Transition

Table 7.1 TRACK/SHIFT Matrix

Table 7.2 Change Adopters at Change Organization

Table 7.3 Leadership Plan for SHIFT at Change Organization

Table 7.4 SHIFT Impact on Defiant Participation

References

Anderson, D. & Ackerman Anderson, L. (2010). *Beyond Change Management: How to Achieve Breakthrough Results Through Conscious Leadership*. Pfeiffer.

Bassett, P. (2011). Change agency leadership. *Independent School*, 1-12.

Beach, L. (2006). *Leadership and the Art of Change*. SAGE Publications.

Bennis, W. (1989). *Why Leaders Can't Lead: The Unconscious Conspiracy Continues*. Jossey-Bass.

Bolman. T.G. & Deal, T.E. (1991). *Reframing Organizations*. Jossey-Bass.

Boyatzis, R., Smith, M. & Van Oosten, E. (2019). *Helping People Change: Coaching with Compassion for Lifelong Learning and Growth*. Harvard Business Review Press.

Braus, Adam. (2019). *Leading Change at Work*. Peripatetic Press.

Brown, R. (2017). *The HST Model for Change: Enhancing the People Side of Organizational Change*. BP Books.

Burke, A. (2008). *Organization Change*. SAGE Publications.

Christensen, C. (2017). *Disrupting Class: How Disruptive Innovation Will Change the Way the World Learns*. McGraw-Hill.

Collins, J. (2001). *Good to Great. Why Some Companies Make the Leap and Others Don't*. Harper Collins Publishers.
Cummings, T. & Worley, C. (2004). *Organization Development and Change*. SouthWestern.

Evans, R. (1996). *The Human Side of School Change: Reform, Resistance, and the Real-Life Problems of Innovation*. Jossey-Bass.

Freire, P. (1973). *Education for Critical Consciousness*. Continuum.

Fullan, M. (2011). *Change Leader: Learning to do What Matters Most*. John Wiley & Sons.

Fullan, M. (2015). *Freedom to Change: Four Strategies to Put Your Inner Drive Into Overdrive*. John Wiley & Sons.

Fullan, M. & Stiegelbauer, S. (1991). *The New Meaning of Educational Change*. Teachers College Press.

Gibbons, P. (2019). *The Science of Organizational Change*. Phronesis Media.

Giroux, H. (2001). *Theory and Resistance in Education: Towards a Pedagogy for the Opposition*. Greenwood Publishing Group.

Grant, A. & Sandberg, S. (2017). *Option B*. Knopf, Borozi Books.

Gregory, C. (2020). *The Five Stages of Grief: An Examination of the Kubler-Ross Model*. Psycom.

Hall, G. & Hord, S. (2006). *Implementing Change: Patterns, Principles, and Potholes* (2nd ed.). Allyn and Bacon.

Heath, C. & Heath, D. (2010). *Switch: How to Change Things When Change is Hard*. Currency.

Kegan, R. & Laskow Lahey, L. (2009). *Immunity to Change: How to Overcome It and Unlock the Potential in Yourself and Your Organization*. Harvard Business Press.

Kotter, J. (2012). *Leading Change*. Harvard Business Review Press.

Lawler, E. & Worley, C. (2006). *Built to Change*. Jossey-Bass.

Little, J. (2014). *Lean Change Management: Innovative Practices for Managing Organizational Change*. Happy Melly Express.

Marris, P. (1986). *Loss and Change*. Routledge & Keagan Paul.

Nolan, J., & Meister, D. G. (2000). *Teachers and Educational Change: The Lived Experience of a Secondary School Restructuring*. SUNY Press.

O'Toole, J. (1995). *Leading Change: Overcoming the Ideology of Comfort and the Tyranny of Custom*. Jossey-Bass.

Piaget, J. (1952). *The Origins of Intelligence in Children*. International Universities Press.

Rock, D. (2008). *SCARF: A Brain-Based Model for Collaborating with and Influencing Others*. Neuro Leadership Journal.

Senge, P. (2014). *The Dance of Change: The Challenges to Sustaining Momentum in a Learning Organization*. Crown Publishing Group.

Schein, E. H. (1992). *Organizational Culture and Leadership: A Dynamic View*. Jossey-Bass.

Shor, I. (2012). *Empowering Education: Critical Teaching for Social Change*. University of Chicago Press.

Snyder, R. (2016). *The Social Cognitive Neuroscience of Leading Organizational Change: Tier 1 Performance Solutions' Guide for Managers and Consultants*. Routledge.

Spallino, J. (2015). *Educators' Response to Change in K-12 Education Factors that Impact Change Efforts*. New Mexico State University, Dissertation.

Wagner, T. (2005). *Change Leadership: A Practical Guide to Transforming Our Schools*. Jossey-Bass.

Warner Burke, W. (2016). *Organizational Change: Theory and Practice*. SAGE Publications.

Watzlawick, P., Weakland, J. & Fisch, R. (2011). *Change: Principles of Problem Formation and Problem Resolution*. W. W. Norton & Company, Inc.

Recommendations for Additional Reading

Collins, J. & Porras, J. (2002). *Built to Last: Successful Habits of Visionary Companies*. Harper Collins.

Fullan, M. (2008). *The Six Secrets of Change: What the Best Leaders do to Help Their Organizations Survive and Thrive*. Jossey-Bass.

Anderson, D. (2017). *Organizational Development: The Process of Leading Organizational Change*. SAGE Publications.

Heath, C. & Heath, D. (2010). *Switch: How to Change Things When Change is Hard*. Currency.

Brown, R. (2017). *The HST Model for Change: Enhancing the People Side of Organizational Change*. BP Books.

Christensen, C. (2017). *Disrupting Class: How Disruptive Innovation Will Change the Way the World Learns*. McGraw-Hill.

Snyder, R. (2016). *The Social Cognitive Neuroscience of Leading Organizational Change: Tier 1 Performance Solutions' Guide for Managers and Consultants*. Routledge.

Warner Burke, W. (2016). *Organizational Change: Theory and Practice*. SAGE Publications

Index

abandonment, 41, 102

Abraham Lincoln, 163

abuse, 9, 41, 43, 53, 62, 109, 115, 146

Adjustment, 10, 11, 61, 72, 98

aggression, 6, 103, 161

Angela Merkel, 163

anxiety, 7, 31, 34, 37, 38, 39, 41, 45, 47, 51, 52, 102, 126, 127

apprehension, 10, 27, 29, 31, 34, 35, 43, 96, 105, 108, 124, 125, 129

automatic responses, 36

Barack Obama, 119

Bill Clinton, 119

bipolar, 7, 34, 102

Black Lives Matter, 161

blended learning, 64, 102

Bryan Stevenson, 116

California, 5, 7, 49, 76, 85, 94, 117, 181

California State University System, 94

career, 7, 39, 97, 102, 103, 112, 113, 117, 118, 123, 135, 139, 147

change, 5, 1, 2, 3, 7, 8, 9, 10, 11, 12, 13, 14, 16, 17, 19, 20, 21, 22, 23, 24, 25, 26, 27, 28, 29, 30, 31, 34, 35, 36, 37, 38, 42, 43, 45, 46, 48, 49, 50, 52, 54, 55, 56, 57, 58, 61, 62, 64, 65, 66, 67, 69, 70, 71, 72, 73, 75, 76, 77, 79, 82, 83, 85, 86, 87, 88, 89, 90, 93, 95, 96, 97, 98, 101, 103, 104, 105, 106, 107, 108, 109, 110, 111, 112, 115, 117, 119, 120, 121, 122, 123, 124, 125, 126, 127, 128, 129, 130, 131, 132, 133, 134, 135, 136, 137, 138, 139, 140, 141, 143, 144, 145, 146, 148, 149, 150, 152, 153, 154, 155, 159, 161, 162, 168, 169, 181

change adopter, 24, 58, 82, 83, 122, 124, 153, 157

change agent, 17, 21, 29, 38, 103, 123, 144, 155

Change Defiants, 25

change management. *See*

change resistance, 5, 30

charter school, 14, 38, 39, 72, 91, 105, 106, 107, 181

charter schools, 70, 72, 105, 106, 181

childhood, 2, 5, 7, 9, 41, 53, 63, 64, 78, 81, 90, 101, 103, 109, 152, 181

classroom, 37, 39, 91

clinical depression, 31

Commitment, 10, 11, 75, 76, 87, 99, 121, 136

communication, 10, 17, 19, 21, 23, 30, 36, 59, 67, 68, 72, 73, 126, 127, 130, 133, 137, 138, 140, 141, 149

Communication, 65, 66, 73, 98, 138

competition, 69, 70, 72

Confusion, 54, 58, 98, 133

Congress, 111, 117

coping mechanism, 7

Counseling, 66, 127

COVID-19 pandemic, 56, 64, 68, 86, 94, 97, 111, 128, 147, 161

creativity, 9, 10, 75, 86, 87, 88, 107, 141, 145, 147

Creativity, 84, 86, 88, 99, 145

culture, 19, 20, 21, 22, 25, 39, 66, 88, 92, 94, 113, 118, 122, 123, 140, 141, 145, 146, 169

curricular change, 13

curriculum, 8, 13, 14, 16, 17, 20, 23, 38, 39, 64, 91, 92, 129, 131, 181

Dave Grohl, 114

defiants, 73, 83, 123

denial, 48, 95

discrimination, 103

Disorientation, 51, 58, 98, 132

divorce, 53, 96, 97, 98, 110, 135, 161

education, 13, 91, 92, 97, 105, 106, 147, 168, 169

educators, 13, 14, 20, 107

emotion, 10, 12, 37, 95, 104, 127

empowerment, 10, 21, 23, 75, 77, 79, 87, 141, 143, 146, 147

Empowerment, 76, 87, 99, 141

England, 85

Equal Justice Initiative, 117

Europe, 85, 102

Evolution, 95, 150

Facebook, 134

fear, 10, 17, 21, 27, 31, 34, 36, 37, 38, 41, 42, 43, 64, 97, 102, 103, 105, 108, 111, 124, 129, 130, 138, 145, 161

fear of the unknown, 10, 27, 31, 37, 43, 64, 97, 103, 105, 108, 124, 129, 130, 138

FedEx, 151, 152, 154

Fred Smith, 154

Frederick Smith, 151

George W. Bush, 151, 152

Grief, 46, 48, 58, 62, 98, 132, 168

grieving, 46, 48, 50, 56, 58, 130, 131, 132, 134, 135, 137

high school, 14, 51, 53, 55, 81, 85, 102, 114, 116, 118

hostility, 103, 127

Howard Shultz, 139, 154

independent study, 14, 38, 66, 91, 97, 102, 105, 106, 181

individualization, 10, 75, 87, 141

Individualization, 79, 87, 99, 144

Interpretive Phenomenological Process (IPA), 17

Jerry Sloan, 112

John McCain, 152

K-12 public school, 13

K-12 schools, 64

Karl Malone, 114

Kathryn Sullivan, 117

Kurt Cobain, 114

Labrador Retriever, 127

Leaders, 1, 29, 129, 134, 152, 167, 171

leadership, 3, 8, 16, 19, 20, 21, 22, 23, 24, 25, 29, 30, 67, 73, 79, 83, 86, 93, 101, 103, 104, 106, 108, 113, 120, 123, 124, 134, 152, 153, 162, 167, 169

liberal, 102

Loss of Control, 40, 44, 98, 127

Louis Vuitton, 147, 154

Malala Yousafzazi, 163

manipulation, 103

marriage, 53, 95, 96, 102, 111, 135

Martin Luther King, 163

middle school, 109

modality, 64, 91, 105, 106, 128, 129, 131

Modeling, 61, 136

Mohandas Gandhi, 163

mountain bike, 35

NASA, 119

Nelson Mandela, 163

New Mexico, 76, 169

Nirvana, 114, 115

online, 13, 14, 16, 38, 39, 56, 57, 64, 73, 94, 102, 106, 128, 129, 130, 134, 149, 152, 181

Oregon, 33, 34

Organize, 132

Origin Response, 9

origins, 5, 1, 2, 3, 7, 8, 9, 10, 11, 12, 22, 24, 28, 29, 31, 39, 42, 43, 44, 58, 61, 72, 82, 87, 96, 101, 103, 104, 106, 107, 108, 110, 112, 113, 114, 115, 117, 118, 119, 120, 121, 122, 124, 126, 127, 129, 130, 132, 133, 134, 135, 136, 139, 140, 141, 142, 143, 147, 149, 150, 152, 153, 155, 159, 161, 162, 181

Parents, 94

Patience, 46

Pedagogies, 181

Peet's Coffee & Tea, 140

planning, 3, 12, 29, 50, 58, 122, 129, 130, 139, 141, 153, 154, 155

psychological exploration, 2

racism, 108, 111, 112, 161

Reflection, 88, 120

Regret, 10, 23, 31, 45, 46, 57, 58, 98, 121, 124, 130, 165

reinforcement, 105, 107, 111, 143, 150, 162

relationships, 19, 20, 35, 39, 41, 52, 57, 65, 98, 122, 126

response to change, 3, 14, 93, 126, 127

Rihanna, 146, 147

roots, 1, 84, 102, 111, 116, 161

Roper v. Simmons, 117

SCARF model, 37

schizophrenia, 7, 34, 102, 110

school, 9, 13, 14, 22, 32, 36, 37, 38, 39, 54, 55, 63, 71, 72, 85, 90, 91, 94, 103, 105, 106, 107, 109, 113, 116, 117, 119, 128, 129, 162, 169, 181

school district, 14

school districts, 72, 94, 105, 106, 128, 162

Sheryl Sandberg, 134

SHIFT, 13, 26, 28, 29, 121, 122, 123, 153, 154, 155, 156, 157, 158, 165, 166

Social Justice, 116

Southern Center for Human Rights, 117

Starbucks Coffee Company, 139

teaching, 14, 91, 128, 169, 181

teaching credentials, 91, 181

Tenacity, 68, 70, 73, 98, 138

tolerance, 20, 27, 46, 57, 82, 133

Tom Petty, 115

TRACK, 10, 12, 13, 17, 22, 23, 26, 27, 28, 29, 43, 57, 72, 87, 121, 153, 155, 165

traits, 20, 109

transformation, 9, 12, 61, 76, 87, 89, 90, 105, 107, 111, 112, 136, 149, 150, 152

trust, 19, 35, 50, 65, 78, 126, 134, 138

turmoil, 9, 11, 27, 41, 44, 55, 62, 65, 76, 86, 89, 92, 102, 104, 105, 106, 108, 111, 129, 137, 157, 161, 162

Turmoil, 10, 23, 31, 43, 62, 98, 121, 124, 165

Utah, 53, 113

Utah Jazz, 113

virtual, 128, 181

vision, 10, 17, 20, 21, 23, 24, 25, 30, 59, 62, 63, 64, 65, 66, 67, 72, 76, 101, 103, 107, 108, 111, 112, 115, 137, 139, 140, 141, 143, 149, 162, 163

Washington Football Team, 152

Xerox, 139

About the Author

Jessica Spallino holds deep origins from her working-class upbringing in Southern California as part of a family of seven. The value of hard work and conscientiousness was ingrained in her throughout her childhood. She grew up in Pomona and then San Dimas, CA, and after several years of exploration, completed a BA from California State University, Northridge when she was 25 years old.

After completing both her single and multiple subject teaching credentials, she skipped the traditional teaching route and went directly into the field of independent study charter schools. Her first experience was at a small school in Oceanside, CA where she worked for 10 years as a curriculum coordinator and program manager, and transitioned the paper-packet model to an online format. After developing multiple new virtual programs there she left to work for the international curriculum company, K12. During her three years there, she helped develop multiple virtual schools throughout CA while she completed a MA in Educational Administration and a Ph.D. in Curriculum with an emphasis on Critical Pedagogies. After experiencing tumultuous change at the small charter school, she wrote her dissertation on K12 Educators' Response to Change and has furthered her study and deepened her curiosity about change dynamics.

After leaving K12, she co-founded her own network of independent study charter schools along with a comprehensive online platform that she now partners with others to implement in their schools. She has a deep passion for supporting change dynamics within her own organization and those seeking help in implementing changes within their own. Her ongoing research and experience have helped her to develop the concept of deeply held origins we all hold that are established primarily throughout the formative years of our lives. She asserts that these origins emerge as deeply held emotions triggered during change experiences and can cause destructive barriers to effectual change. She affirms that developing the awareness and appropriate treatment for these origins can simplify and therefore empower the change process, potentially limiting destructive change resistant behavior.

Jessica currently resides in Southern California with her family, and is writing a second book on the development of her own organization and the story of its progression within a volatile and changing environment. She also consults for those in need of change management and origin support.

www.ingramcontent.com/pod-product-compliance
Lightning Source LLC
Chambersburg PA
CBHW031625210526
45464CB00004B/1755